PRAISE FOR *THE RE-ENCHANTMENT*

"*The Re-Enchantment* is full of magic, insight, and profound realizations about the nature of spirit and life. Hank Wesselman is a master teacher of shamanism. Re-enchant your life by reading this excellent book!"

JUDITH ORLOFF, MD
author of *Second Sight*

"Hank Wesselman is a genuine and engaging storyteller who blends his scientific wisdom with his experience with shamanism from a place of heart. In *The Re-Enchantment* . . . Hank is courageous and touches on subjects from which other authors have shied away. He has created an important book for modern day shamanic practitioners and vision seekers alike."

SANDRA INGERMAN, MA
author of *Soul Retrieval* and *Walking in Light: The Everyday Empowerment of Shamanic Life*; coauthor (with Hank Wesselman) of the award-winning *Awakening to the Spirit World*

"One of the curses of our modern world is the assumption that we must choose between science and spirituality, reason and intuition, objectivity and subjectivity. This false choice has led us to a critical threshold in which it is uncertain whether our species will survive. That is why Dr. Hank Wesselman's vision is so important. [His] personal experiences and vision transcend the suffocating limitations of materialism that now threaten our future . . . If we respond to Dr. Wesselman's message, we humans will not only survive, but thrive."

LARRY DOSSEY, MD
author of *One Mind: How Our Individual Mind Is Part of a Greater Consciousness and Why It Matters*

D0019244

"If you have felt that something is missing in our endless discussions of what's wrong in our world, you may be feeling the need that Dr. Wesselman presents so convincingly: to re-enchant both nature and ourselves, to embrace the new mysteries coming into being and to overcome our spiritual blindness."

TOM COWAN
author of *Fire in the Head: Shamanism and the Celtic Spirit* and
Yearning for the Wind: Celtic Reflections on Nature and the Soul

"Dr. Hank Wesselman has written a provocative book on how we as spiritual beings put reality together with luminosity and with a new vision. To me, a book is a promise to readers that your integrity as a writer will be impeccable. Dr. Wesselman has kept his promise."

LYNN ANDREWS
author of the *New York Times* and internationally
bestselling Medicine Woman Series

"In *The Re-Enchantment*, Hank Wesselman helps us to find songlines for our modern lives. Drawing on a lifetime of scholarship and deep shamanic practice, he invites us to follow a path of direct experience of the sacred. . . . You'll be thrilled by his accounts of his personal awakenings to the deeper reality."

ROBERT MOSS
bestselling author of *Conscious Dreaming*, *The Secret History
of Dreaming*, and *The Boy Who Died and Came Back*

"*The Re-Enchantment* by Hank Wesselman is a triumphant achievement that reveals insights into our natural, spiritual birthrights and expertly teaches us to open ourselves to the elusive Great Mystery, the guiding force for a true life of flow and harmony . . . I highly recommend it."

ITZHAK BEERY
author of *The Gift of Shamanism* and *Shamanic Transformations* and the publisher of Shaman Portal (shamanportal.org)

"Those in search of epiphanies, the kind that generate action and change, will find in this book a treasure trove. It is filled with insights that may draw readers to 'ego-shattering, mind-expanding, and soul-enhancing awareness.' It's a 'Must have!' book for anyone seriously seeking life-altering change."

NICKI SCULLY
author of *Alchemical Healing*, and coauthor of *The Shamanic Mysteries of Egypt* and *The Union of Isis and Thoth*

THE RE-ENCHANTMENT

ALSO BY HANK WESSELMAN

THE SPIRITWALKER TRILOGY

Spiritwalker: Messages from the Future

Medicinemaker: Mystic Encounters on the Shaman's Path

Visionseeker: Shared Wisdom from the Place of Refuge

The Journey to the Sacred Garden:
A Guide to Traveling in the Spiritual Realms

Spirit Medicine: A Guide to Healing in the Sacred Garden
(with Jill Kuykendall)

Awakening to the Spirit World: The Shamanic Path
of Direct Revelation (with Sandra Ingerman)

The Bowl of Light: Ancestral Wisdom from a Hawaiian Shaman

Little Ruth Reddingford and the Wolf (for children)

AUDIO AND VIDEO LEARNING

The Spiritwalker Teachings: Journeys for the Modern Mystic
(with Jill Kuykendall)

The Shaman's Path

THE
RE-ENCHANTMENT

A SHAMANIC PATH
TO A LIFE OF WONDER

HANK WESSELMAN, PhD

sounds true
BOULDER, COLORADO

Sounds True, Inc.
Boulder, CO 80306

Cover design by Rachael Murray
Cover painting by Judith Currelly
Book design by Beth Skelley

Printed in Canada

Library of Congress Cataloging-in-Publication Data
Names: Wesselman, Henry Barnard, author.
Title: The re-enchantment : a Shamanic path to a life of wonder /
   Hank Wesselman, PhD.
Description: Boulder, CO : Sounds True, 2016. | Includes bibliographical
   references.
Identifiers: LCCN 2016011004 (print) | LCCN 2016037325 (ebook) |
   ISBN 9781622035595 | ISBN 9781622036332
Subjects: LCSH: Shamanism. | Spiritual life.
Classification: LCC BF1621 .W39 2016 (print) | LCC BF1621 (ebook) |
   DDC 201/.44—dc23
LC record available at https://lccn.loc.gov/2016011004

Ebook ISBN 978-1-62203-633-2

10 9 8 7 6 5 4 3 2 1

This book is offered with my deep gratitude and great affection to my beautiful lady, Jill Kuykendall, who has shared her life with me as my wife, my best friend, and the mother of our children, and who has been my most endearing, loving, and wise teacher for more than forty years. Her kindness, her great good humor, and her generosity have served as the foundation for our family, our relationship, and for all that followed.

The mysteries have been securely preserved by each cultural tradition of each land, and each will now be closely associated to their restoration. This cultural revitalization movement will form the home for these ancient mysteries as well as provide each culture (and each individual) with their seat of initiation.

HALE KEALOHALANI MAKUA, Hawaiian kahuna elder

Our practice is not to clear up the mystery.
It is to make the mystery clear.

ROBERT AITKEN RŌSHI, Zen master, from a talk given in Hawai'i, October 1987

It is high time we realized that it is pointless to praise the light and preach it if nobody can see it. It is much more needful to teach people the art of seeing. For it is obvious that far too many people are incapable of establishing a connection between the sacred figures and their own psyche: they cannot see to what extent the equivalent images are lying dormant in their own unconscious.

CARL JUNG, *Psychology and Alchemy* (vol. 12 of *The Collected Works of C. G. Jung*)
(R. F. C. Hull, translator)

Contents

Introduction

I am a scientist, an evolutionary biologist, and a paleoanthropologist who has been involved in the search for evidence of the mystery of human evolution for about forty-five years. I do not consider myself a New Ager, a theologian, or a priest, nor am I a Buddhist, although I walked that path for many years and still value it. My territory as a researcher is prehistory—a vast, largely empty expanse of time that extends from the beginnings of written language perhaps five thousand years ago back toward the origins of humanity many millions of years beyond that. I have always been intensely curious about everything, and in line with my scientific investigations of the past, I became interested, even compelled, to explore the nature of my self, my humanity, and the nature of the great mystery of existence in the present.

My expeditionary field research in the fossil beds of eastern Africa's Great Rift Valley brought me into repeated contact with indigenous tribal peoples, who still have inspired visionaries known as shamans. This connection was pivotal for me because I sometimes found myself drawn spontaneously into unsought visions and lucid dreams, and my discussions with these traditional people helped to explain and give context for my dreams and visions. These visions tended to be periodic and were much like daydreams, but very, very real. They often happened when I was immersed in the natural world for extended periods, and in response, I, a native New Yorker, was inexorably drawn onto the ancient mystical path of the shaman. I would learn—as revealed in my other books—that this visionary ability appears to run in my family.

In my investigations of what I came to think of as "the Mystery," I stumbled into the realization that there is a new spiritual complex coming into being in the Western world, a mystical mosaic drawn from many traditions and many cultures, one that has the potential to replace or at least refresh all of our current mainstream religions with new perceptions and new insights. There are many spiritual paths through which this awakening is happening, and one of the most powerful and luminous is that of the shaman. The worldview of the shaman and the direct revelations that may be accessed through the shaman's expanded understanding of how we and reality are really put together are contributing to this new spiritual assemblage.

I am well aware of those ethnic purists who proclaim with fervor that the word *shaman* can only be applied to tribal mystics of the Tungusic-speaking peoples of Siberia. However, allow me to note that the word *shaman* was chosen by professional anthropologists and ethnographers in the twentieth century and given a precise definition to accurately describe tribal mystics who perform spiritual practices on behalf of their communities, usually on a part-time basis. Such practitioners are very widespread on planet Earth today, and despite different appellations used to describe these visionaries, there is a remarkable congruence in their practice and in their worldview. Accordingly, it can be observed that the shaman is a universal figure found in some form in every culture and that our Western use of the term *shaman* is valid.

In this book, we will consider the shaman as an archetype for a particular kind of human: a woman or a man who can serve their communities as a mediator between the outer world of things seen and the inner worlds of things hidden. And we will talk about what that means. We will consider the worldview of the shaman and will visit various visionary perspectives, such as those of the Druids, the Tibetans, the American Indians, the Gnostics, the ancient Egyptians, and the Eastern Orthodox Christians. Yet our investigations will not be another academic compilation of the esoteric belief systems of this cultural group or that. Rather, we will investigate some of the visionary mystical perceptions that are being achieved by everyday folks like ourselves on an ongoing basis.

We will also consider how the shaman's perception of reality is being reworked by modern Western mystics into a new form in response to who we are today and who we are becoming. The shift in our cultural mythos—the pattern of basic values and attitudes of a people—that is going on right now happens only once or twice in a thousand years. This book will explore this phenomenon and look at the beliefs, values, and trends that are part of the new spiritual complex that is coming into being. As it does, our understanding will be enhanced by encounters with the legendary psychologist Carl Jung.

It is noteworthy that this spiritual reawakening is occurring among many who are in social and professional positions from which it is possible to influence the larger societies' ideals and trends. You, the reader, are most likely among the increasing numbers of spiritual seekers who are investigating the full potentials of our uniquely human consciousness and in the process learning to balance the functions of mind, body, and spirit. You represent a distinct and growing cultural subgroup that holds a set of beliefs and values different from those of the general public—beliefs that cross socioeconomic borders and values that reflect the influence of non-Western traditions currently being molded into the new spiritual complex. This book will discuss some of these beliefs and values, as well as the social context in which they are taking form.

As you will see, the initial stages of our individual spiritual unfolding inevitably involve the experience of enchantment early in life. As we move into our lives as active participants, the enchantment may withdraw for a time, and then sometimes, mysteriously, it may reappear, often through a powerful connection with nature. This re-enchantment through nature, in my opinion, is predictable, even inevitable, because nature is where the juice is. I'm talking about the life force that breathes essence and wonder into our world and into our selves.

In these investigations of the ancient, yet curiously modern, tradition of shamanism, perhaps you will discover that you are one of those worthies who possesses the gift of spirit vision. Believe it or not, an extraordinarily large sector of our population does, although many do not know that they have it.

As a scientist, I always kept journals while I was in the field, and the following chapters are like field reports from a life that has been lived like an adventure. In these chapters, I offer some of my discoveries and insights about the "New Mysteries" that seem to be coming into being in response to our need for them. These narratives are much like the song lines that for tens of thousands of years have guided the Australian Aboriginal peoples across their vast lands under huge skies—songs that were sung as they trekked, songs that revealed the way to this water-hole or that sacred place or campsite, songs that also guided them across the dusty borderlands of the Dreamtime. It is my hope that the revelations within these narratives may enhance your own path of discovery out there on the trail, where you may encounter initiatory experiences that can lead you to that which you are destined to become.

My invitation to you is quite simple: Would you like to engage in an absolutely extraordinary experience—an expedition of spiritual unfolding through which you can begin to move toward who and what your destiny holds out to you? Because that is what re-enchantment is all about.

The Enchantment
and Re-Enchantment

I have now been walking on the magical mystery road of life for seventy-five years. The magic and the mystery began in my childhood in the early 1940s, but I had no understanding of what was going on then, nor any clear idea of that for which I had signed up. Yet I remember the first time I experienced being enchanted. Perhaps you do too.

In my case, I was about three or four years old, and my family and I lived in an apartment on New York's Upper East Side. One day, my mother took me to Central Park. I remember staring up at the trees from my stroller, taking them all in, and suddenly I had a deep insight. I saw them as living beings like myself, yet different. And then there were the pigeons on the sidewalks, bobbing and cooing, mobbing and hassling each other for the breadcrumbs my mother spread out for them. They were also living beings like myself, yet different.

And then there was the squirrel. It was just your average, everyday gray squirrel. It was perched on the gray trunk of a large beech tree, its curled fluffy tail twitching with alert intensity above its back, its liquid jet-black eye staring straight into my soul. My mother gave me a peanut. In my innocence I held it out. The squirrel, conditioned by countless generations of curious children, approached tentatively, jumped onto the edge of the stroller, and looked deep into my eyes for a long moment. And then it snatched the peanut in one swift gesture from my trembling little fingers, retreating like a flash onto the tree trunk where it shredded the shell and ate the peanut with great gusto. Then it returned for another.

In those moments, I was enchanted. It was as though a spell had been cast over me. I had been entranced by none other than Mother Nature herself through a rather hyper furry ambassador. This initial experience remains with me to this day, and there was more.

There was the zoo. My mother took me there often. The sights and sounds and smells remain with me still—the hippopotamus in its small depressing concrete pool of murky greenish water stained with hippo poo, the crocodile lazing on its cement embankment in deep meditation, the birds shrieking with joyous abandon in their aviaries, the sea lions cavorting in their outdoor pond accompanied always by the odor of fish.

And then one day, one very strange enchanted day, I saw a beast of incomparable beauty in a cage. It was a leopard. It was such an extraordinarily exquisite being that I still remember the wonder and intensity I felt in response to our meeting. I say "our meeting" for that was exactly what it was. As I watched this gorgeous creature pacing in tight, ever-narrowing circles behind the bars, I was spellbound, entranced by its beauty, yes, but also by its power and by my own intuitive perception that within its graceful spotted body, a great will lay imprisoned.

I didn't know what this meant, of course, but the world as I knew it drifted in those moments, and where it drifted to I do not know, but the leopard and I found ourselves together in a place of utter calm, a shadowy blue place of deep magic where there were no bars. As I watched, the veil over its green gaze silently lifted, and the leopard looked deeply into my soul.

And something happened.

Looking back across the years, I reach for that moment, and it eludes me. Yet it was on that cold, foggy winter day at the zoo that something definitely happened—something that in retrospect I now know had to do with my enchantment. From that time forward, that leopard became my imaginary spirit friend. It was with me whenever I turned my attention in its direction. Sometimes it appeared in my mind's eye as entirely catlike, and at others it would morph to become a curious composite of human-animal that stood upright on two legs that I thought of as "the leopard man." More than forty years later I would create a painting of it that graces the cover of one of my books.

Interestingly, in my so-called inner fantasy life, the leopard man would not enter my apartment building. He liked to stick to the bushes in the park. What I didn't know then was that leopards are ambush hunters and they prefer to engage in covert operations. But when I went to the park with my mother or my au pair, the leopard man was always there waiting for me. Perhaps our clandestine relationship and our imaginal adventures contributed to the reactivation of an ancient aspect of my soul that I had no idea existed at that time. And there was more.

With adolescence in the 1950s, my inner world was steamrollered by puberty, by my growing fascination with what Zorba the Greek called "the female of the species," and by material culture at large. In response, perhaps, the sense of magic withdrew, but interestingly the mystery remained. When I was out in nature, in the garden, at the pond in the woods, in the park, at the beach, in the mountains, or on the wooded university campus, the mystery was around me as a definite yet elusive presence, and I always had a sense that something I could not see or even understand was just *there*. I also had a clear perception that it, whatever *it* was, was always aware of me too.

I knew nothing of mysticism or enchantment or visionary experience in those days, but not surprisingly, I have always loved being out in nature. And when I finally read Henry David Thoreau's *Walden*, I knew exactly what he was talking about.

Perhaps this is why my college studies in the 1960s at the University of Colorado at Boulder propelled me toward becoming a biological scientist. My inner visionary was on hold, and upon graduation I did a two-year stint as a science teacher with the U.S. Peace Corps in western Nigeria where I connected with indigenous spirituality for the first time among the Yoruba peoples. Although everyone I met was either Christian or Muslim, there was also a deep, underlying animist tribal religion that existed, one that was imported into the Americas with the slave trade, becoming known as Macumba, Candomblé, or Umbanda in Brazil, Vodou in Haiti, Obea in Jamaica, and Santeria in Cuba. I would discover years later that while I lived among the Yorubas, I attracted the attention of some of the spirits they call *orisha*, yet I didn't fully understand what this meant at that time.

In my postgraduate studies and scientific professional life that followed in the 1970s, I traversed the entangled trails of evolutionary and environmental biology with relation to paleontology and anthropology. I was in search of insights into the living world of the biosphere on the one hand and, more specifically, the evolution of life preserved as fossils in the lithosphere on the other.

I fell in with an anthropology professor named F. Clark Howell at the University of California at Berkeley who was then director of the American half of the Omo Research Expedition in Ethiopia (the other half was French). In 1971, he graciously invited me into the field, where my research projects involved the excavation and recovery of microvertebrate fossils—bats, insectivores (shrews), rodents, lagomorphs (rabbits), mole rats, galagos, mongooses, and other small mammals that tend to be very habitat specific. Through my analysis of these fossils, I attempted to reconstruct the paleoenvironments of important prehistoric early man sites at the time they were laid down millions of years ago. I also tried to understand the inner workings of the evolutionary process within lineages of fossil animals across time, seeing how they had changed and trying to discern why. This work led me into my scientific investigations of what I came to refer to as "the Mystery" and eventually earned me a doctoral degree in anthropology. I still do this work today.

ENCOUNTERS WITH THE MYSTERY

In the early 1970s, I was living for months at a time in a tented safari camp out in the fossil beds of the Lower Omo Valley in southwestern Ethiopia, and I remember having spontaneous, unsought dreamlike experiences that were definitely odd. They often happened at night, but they also occurred during the day when I was fully awake. They were so extraordinarily real that they got my attention. It was as though I was watching films, but I was aware that I was watching them. Through these direct and immediate experiences, I was inevitably drawn into the Mystery.

There was one episode that contributed greatly to what I now perceive as my re-enchantment in my early thirties.

I was involved in excavating a paleontological (fossil-bearing) site that had been dated by geochronology (potassium-argon dating) at about three million years or a little older, a site that had revealed the fossilized remains of early hominids still in the process of becoming human. There were also fossils of various other animals that were their contemporaries—ancestral giraffes, gazelles, buffalos, baboons, fish, turtles, hippos, crocodiles, and the assorted carnivores that preyed upon them.

I was working with a small team of African tribal men. Two of them were Wakamba tribesmen from Kenya named Muthoka and Kaumbulu; the other, a member of the local Dassanetch tribe, was named Lokiriakwanga, but everyone called him Atiko. I had been told that Atiko was a shaman. In fact, he was rumored to be a crocodile-whisperer in that he could communicate with the immense crocodilians that inhabited the Omo River at that time. It was said he could even swim across the river immune to the enormous reptilian predators that resided there. Having seen them myself, I understood this was no small thing.

I didn't speak a word of Atiko's language, nor did he of mine, but friendship has a language of its own, and with repeated and ongoing contact over several field seasons we became very close. I could speak a little Swahili by then, above which, or perhaps below which, we had a system of nonverbal communication that worked very well. He always knew exactly what to do without my telling him, and in reverse, I came to suspect that he had a profound influence on me, although I was largely unaware of this at that time.

One blazing hot day, around noon in mid-August, we were excavating fossil beds near the great silt-laden Omo River, which drains the Ethiopian highlands to the north and flows into Lake Turkana in Kenya to the south. The eroded desert landscape under the vast pale sky was surreal. The ground was shimmering with heat, and we were preparing to go back to camp for lunch. I had been aware for several days, usually at odd moments, of a curious feeling that would come over me—the sense that I was being watched by something. We were out in the remote, whispering lands of eastern Africa where there are lions and leopards, hyenas and Cape buffalo, all of whom are dangerous. So this awareness—that I was being watched—was concerning.

On this day, my mind was drifting, hypnotized by the heat and the general boredom of what we were doing, when the sense of being watched suddenly flared. I stood up slowly, dusting myself off and observing my immediate surroundings carefully from under the brim of my bush hat. Muthoka and Kaumbulu were packing the excavation equipment into the Land Rover as Atiko, the Dassanetch shaman, was looking off to one side with some intensity.

As my eyes slid slowly in that direction, I suddenly saw something with my peripheral vision. It was big, about the same height as me, and as I looked directly at it, it seemed to step through a rip in the fabric of the air, which was then zipped closed from the other side, leaving a momentary wrinkle in the space between us. I was startled. As I considered the nature of this unusual visual phenomenon, I was left with a curious certainty. Whatever it was, it had spots. I had definitely seen spots!

I turned my attention toward Atiko, who was now watching me with an alert expression on his thin dark face, and I asked him in Swahili, "Atiko, what was that?" The shaman smiled, revealing his tobacco-stained front teeth. I knew then that he had seen it, and he knew that I had seen it. He simply pointed to the exact spot in the air where it had been and said a single word: *shaitani,* the Swahili word for spirit.

In those days I worshipped only at the altar of science. I was not one of those worthies who had sat at the knees of the wisdom masters for decades, praying and meditating and hoping for visions and transcendent experiences, and I wasn't prepared to consider the existence of spirits. But this incident, and the ones that followed, would haunt me for years, and shortly thereafter, Atiko bent a simple honey-colored brass tribal bracelet around my wrist. It remains there to this day, a token of our long-ago friendship and perhaps of something else—something that he saw in me. It became a talisman connecting me, a native New Yorker, to the indigenous world and to our communal, ancient tribal past.

❁

During that same field season in the Omo Valley, another strange experience happened to me.

It was another hot afternoon, and my mentor, Clark Howell, and I had driven out of our field camp in one of the expedition Land Rovers to hunt for the large Grant's gazelles to provide fresh meat for the camp kitchen. With us was Don Johanson, the same man who two years later would discover Lucy, the now famous fossilized partial skeleton at Hadar, in the Afar tribal lands to the north. Don was one of Clark's graduate students at that time and my tent mate for part of that field season.

There was a large clay pan surrounded by acacia woodlands about five miles north of camp, and we headed in that direction, driving cross-country between towering termite chimneys before entering the woodlands. When we emerged, the flat expanse of dusty, cracked earth of the pan stretched before us several miles across. During the rainy season, the pan would fill with a shallow sheet of water, becoming a place of great proliferation for both plants and animals. Now it was bone dry, and the dark acacia woodlands that bordered its edges were largely leafless, pulsing with heat and shrouded by dust. It was often there that we found large herds of gazelle and sometimes oryx.

The hunt was successful. As we headed back across the pan with a gazelle and several guinea fowl in the back of the vehicle, we saw in the middle of the pan a whitening orb that at first glance looked like an old dried gourd. Clark slowed our vehicle to a stop and turned the engine off without a word. The three of us got out and walked back across the soft crunchy earth. There on the sunbaked lake bed was a human cranium, and it was fairly fresh.

Don, Clark, and I stood there in the glare and breathless heat of afternoon and stared at the skull in silence. Then Clark reached down and picked it up, gingerly turning it this way and that, noting that a cheekbone and a mastoid process were missing, probably gnawed off by jackals. He shook it, and the shrunken, blackened brain bumped around inside the cranium. There were holes pecked into ceilings of the fragile eye sockets by probing beaks, he pointed out. Perhaps some vulture with a taste for brains had taken it up high and dropped it, he said, hoping the fall would break it open. But the pan was soft and crumbly. I looked around carefully. No other remains. Just the head.

He passed it to me. I smelled the sweet aroma of decaying carrion as I examined the last leathery shreds of sun-dried muscle still hooked on. The bone was greasy with fat. I looked at the delicate facial features as my fingertips traced the parietal prominences, and I perceived the cranium as female. All her teeth were in place and with no decay. They were quite worn, revealing a woman in her thirties, perhaps. I had been told by Serge Tornay, a French social anthropologist doing ethnographic field research in a tribal village to the west called Kibish, that the Nyangatom people who lived in this region did not bury their dead but left them out on the plains to be recycled by hyenas, vultures, and jackals. Whether this was true or not I did not know.

As a paleoanthropologist, I have handled my share of human bones, so this was not an unusual experience for me. But what happened next was. As I looked full into her empty eye sockets, I began to hear a strange whispering sound, like rushing water, but a quick glance to the side revealed only the shimmering emptiness of the arid land. I looked back at the face before me and began to see curious sparkling spots of light, and in the next moment my carefully cultivated scientific detachment simply vanished.

The vacant eyes seemed to merge with the barren land, creating a perceived field that progressed into an ever-expanding sense of emptiness in which, curiously, there was still something. Then, in the same heartbeat, that "something" vanished too, whereupon I experienced an utter and total separation from all the levels on which I had been living my life. My involvement with academia and with science, my connections with friends and even with family, these simply disappeared, and in their place, an awesome, overwhelming vastness opened up before me.

I could see my hands holding the skull, and I was still aware of my surroundings, yet I was also perceiving this unbelievable immensity. It was like an ocean of light in which there were uncountable numbers of sparkling yellow-golden spots or dots. This field of moving points simply absorbed me until it was as though I no longer existed. There was only the vastness—and it was beautiful beyond belief.

Don reached out at that moment and took the cranium from my hands, and suddenly all was as it had been. I was back. The sound was gone. Where exactly had I been? What had I seen?

Clark was watching me curiously, his expressive blue eyes filled with a sudden concern.

"Are you all right?" he asked.

I turned and smiled at him, nodding in a semi-distracted way even as my mind reeled. To cover my confusion, I turned and walked back to the Land Rover and took a pull on the canvas water bag hanging from the outside mirror. I splashed water on my face and looked carefully around, taking in details, feeling the sunlight like a force on the skin of my arms and hands and face, smelling the odor of the dust and my own sweat, recovering my sense of control and place, re-establishing a grasp on what was real.

I looked out across the clay pan to the dark line of trees in the far distance to the south, and, unexpectedly, my consciousness expanded once again. There was something there—something watching me from the cover of the trees. I could feel its attention fastened upon me beyond any doubt. Despite the heat, my skin prickled into goose bumps. What could it be? A side of me stepped back and wondered if I was starting to go crazy out there in the bush after several months' isolation from so-called civilization. I recalled my earlier sense of being watched at the site. Was I another anthropologist gone *troppo* in the tropics? I considered this thought briefly and wondered exactly what *troppo* meant. It was suddenly terribly important.

My carefully crafted, well-traveled veneer reapplied itself at this point, and I looked around at my compatriots just as Don put the skull back down on the ground. I was normal once again. Clark and Don walked back to where I was standing and got back into the Land Rover. I joined them, and we returned to camp in silence.

When we went to the river later in the day to bathe and draw water for the camp, that same sense of being watched came into my awareness. I glanced around in the softening light but failed to see anything out of the ordinary.

I looked toward the brown river. There was only a hamerkop, a small, dusky brown water bird halfway between a heron and a stork. It had short legs, a curious crest on the back of its head, and a croaky, mournful voice. It seemed to be doing a walking meditation back and forth at the river's edge. It paused thoughtfully, as though it was staring at its own reflection in the water, and then it resumed walking.

My attention was suddenly drawn to the hamerkop. I studied the bird abstractedly and wondered why my focus was directed there. I remembered that some African peoples regard the hamerkop with considerable deference, perceiving it as a powerful being associated with omens and portents. For them, it is a bird identified with shamans and diviners. In myth, this bird is also associated with rainmaking and thunderstorms. Accordingly, it is often known as the Lightning Bird. Among the peoples of southern Africa, it is believed that sometimes the Lightning Bird takes it upon itself to appear among them in human form.[1]

All this passed through my mind as I watched the bird. I was aware that my sense of being watched was not coming from it. The sense was coming from the trees beside the river. I had no sense of alarm or danger, just a sense of being observed by something—a flat, neutral presence of some sort just there at the edge of my mind.

It was during that same field season that I began to have very odd dreams at night. One night, I was in my safari tent, and in turning over on my bed, I found myself bumping against something hard. Upon opening my eyes, I discovered I was up against the ridge pole under the peak of the double roof of the tent. To say I was startled would be an understatement. I turned over and looked down, and there below me was my body lying on my bed. Then suddenly, I was back in my body, wondering what I had just experienced. (I might add that I was not taking any mind-altering substances, and we were hundreds of miles cross-country from the nearest cold beer.)

On another starry night, I had another experience of being out of my body and discovered I could slip through the screened doorway of my tent without zipping it open. There I was, hovering above the camp, seeing with a curious enhanced perspective. I could see everything in great detail, and each of the nineteen safari tents that made up the camp was outlined with a strange halo of light. I discovered I could maneuver myself around in this state, floating above the scene below me, drifting here and there according to my wishes.

As I rose higher and higher, I could see the Ethiopian highlands to the east and the mountain called Nkalabong to the north. The vast, empty, surreal landscapes of the fossil beds near the camp stretched down toward Lake Turkana to the south, and there was the long volcano to the west that Atiko called Kuraz. It was as though I could see in all directions at once. And during the entire experience, my body was infused with the most extraordinary sensation that verged on the ecstatic.

These out-of-body experiences continued. They were spontaneous in that I didn't intend them, nor did I understand what was actually happening to me at that time, and I didn't quite know what to make of them. Then one morning, after another long nocturnal flight over the camp, I was brushing my teeth at the water tank before breakfast, and my Wakamba friend Kaumbulu walked up to me. He looked at me strangely and said, "Hey, Mr. Hank. What were you doing flying over my tent last night?" I simply stared at him dumbfounded, and he laughed his crazy laugh and walked away. He never elaborated, yet what he'd said got my attention. I gathered this was not the sort of thing you can talk about with your scientific colleagues, so I made cryptic notes to myself in my field journal and just left it at that.

The Return of the Enchantment

In reviewing these initial experiences, I realize that they were facilitated by my being immersed in nature for months at a time. I believe now that this immersion had something to do with my re-enchantment.

Ten years later, I found myself attending a weekend workshop in Berkeley led by a fellow anthropologist named Michael Harner. I had never taken a workshop before, and this one was focused on the way of the shaman. I supposed I would get something out of it for teaching future anthropology classes. However, there was also something else—that nagging memory of what had happened during those days out in the fossil beds and those nights in the camp.

As part of the weekend's experiential exercises, Harner asked us to team up with someone in the group whom we didn't already know. Then he directed us to engage in a visionary shamanic journey into the spirit worlds to find a "helping spirit" to be in service for that other person. I was very uncertain; this exercise seemed like New Age woo-woo to me, but I found myself partnered with a slender, attractive young woman with dark eyes and long dark hair. Her name was Sandra Ingerman, and at that time she was a graduate student in counseling psychology at the California Institute of Integral Studies in San Francisco.

I lay on my back on the floor in the dark next to this woman, listening to Harner beating his drum in a monotonous rhythm to help us alter our consciousness. I was wondering what in God's name I was doing there when suddenly Sandra sat up next to me, gave me an intense look, and leaned over, her long hair drifting across my face. She placed her cupped hands and mouth on my chest and blew into my thorax—not once but several times. A strange sense of warmth percolated through my being, accompanied, surprisingly, by something dimly remembered. I couldn't quite grasp it. Then Sandra helped me to sit up and blew her breath into the top of my head. It was a goose-bump moment.

When Harner stopped drumming and the lights came up, Sandra shared what she had experienced in her shamanic journey. In projecting her conscious awareness (journeying) into the dreaming of the shamanic Lower Worlds of nature, she had encountered a being who revealed to her that it was one of my old allies—one I had forgotten about, one that wanted to come back into my life. When she described it, I reacted with shock. It was my imaginal friend, the leopard man. I hadn't thought of him in perhaps thirty years. How had Sandra known about him? This experience got my attention and something shifted within me—something that would usher me into the next stage of my life.

Although I didn't know it then, it was a classic shamanic experience of re-empowerment. It was the next step of my re-enchantment, a reconnection with the inner worlds of spirit that had been part of my childhood. That reconnection enabled an entirely new level of awareness to take form in my life from that time on. I came to understand that it involved the reactivation of one of my birthrights, a revitalization of my soul that led me back onto the path of my destiny, and my life has never been the same. This was how I discovered that I am a spirit dreamer, or as revealed in my other books, a spiritwalker.

I am now at an age and stage where my mind often wanders back across the path that I have walked for all these years, allowing me to reconsider those insights and revelations that I stumbled across along the trail. For stumbling was very much my way. I wasn't seeking "It," whatever It was. It simply seemed to seek me, and I just allowed myself to stumble into It. And yet as I say this to you, the reader, allow me to also proclaim that I am still not sure what It is. But I am absolutely certain that It is. I continue to think of It simply and forever as the Mystery.

The writer and Zen master Peter Matthiessen put it this way in his classic book about his experiences in Africa, *The Tree Where Man Was Born:* "Lying back against these ancient rocks of Africa, I am content. The great stillness in these landscapes that once made me restless seeps into me day by day, and with it the unreasonable feeling that I have found what I was searching for without ever having discovered what it was."[2]

Having had my own long immersions in the African bush across many years, I know exactly what he is talking about.

In sharing these accounts with you, I am extending you an invitation to re-experience something from your childhood, perhaps something that you possessed before your life took over. I invite you to reconnect with that sense of wonder you may have felt in response to a blue-sky, yellow-sun summer morning, the grass glistening with dew, butterflies hovering around the flowers in the garden. Or maybe it was a trip to the park, a visit to the zoo, a walk in the forest, a day at the beach, or the moon over the ocean that triggered that wonder.

That sense of wonder was and is one of your birthrights, one that may enable you to see more deeply into the outer world of things seen, as well as into the inner worlds of things hidden. I slowly came to the awareness that these worlds are always there for us. It is simply a matter of tuning into the right frequency and paying attention to what happens next. It is a matter of allowing ourselves to be re-enchanted.

Shamanism and the Seat of Initiation

During the years when I was living and working among traditional tribal peoples, I learned that when an individual begins to have visions such as those I have described, it is usually regarded as a sign that they are destined to become a shaman. Mythology reveals that such experiences serve as catalysts that encourage us to grow beyond the known and engage in an adventurous quest into the unknown, into the worlds of things hidden. This quest is known to mythologists as "the hero's journey," and they say that we are all engaged with our own version of the journey through the life games that we choose to play. (More on this below.)

The heroes—in this case, the ones who will become visionaries—are those people who decide to respond to that call to adventure. Once we step onto this path, we are precipitated into the life stage that the Hawaiian elder Hale Makua called "the seat of initiation." Makua, as he was generally known, often referred to this as "the school of hard knocks" because it is during this stage that our life may unravel in truly spectacular ways, often in a very short period of time. For the inspired visionary, these life experiences, though hard, are pivotal, because in order to acquire and develop the power of spirit vision, we must first experience authentic initiation.

When we sit in the seat of initiation as emerging visionaries, the journey can be facilitated by training with accomplished shamans in order to deepen and further our ability into a permanent and enduring capacity in which we may experience at will the spirits and the realities they inhabit. This is what happened for me when I encountered the tribal man Atiko in Ethiopia and then ten years later Michael Harner and Sandra Ingerman in Berkeley. There were also many others who came into my life during my initiations.

I should mention that there are also those who are solely "spirit trained," yet if they are without the guidance of an experienced and authentic teacher, their spiritual emergence can look a lot like a spiritual emergency—like mental illness. My discussions with Makua about this phenomenon are included in chapter 12.

In my other conversations with Makua over the years, some of which are recorded in *The Bowl of Light: Ancestral Wisdom from a Hawaiian Shaman*, he often observed that from the perspective of the spiritual seeker, the seat of initiation involves

> those circumstances that will raise and expand the
> consciousness of humankind, for these circumstances
> alone will produce the betterment of the individual,
> the family, the culture, and the environment,
> accompanied by a continuing, unfolding spiritual
> recognition. It is through the seat of initiation
> that we approach the goal of deepened intelligence
> through which our consciousness expands and our
> connection with the greater whole is enhanced.[1]

Shamanism provides the perfect vehicle for approaching this goal of deepened intelligence and experiencing ourselves as an interface between the worlds of things seen and the worlds of things hidden. The whole purpose of shamanic practice is to turn mirrors into windows. And the quest? That depends on the life games we choose to play. This brings up what some have called the Master Game.

THE GREAT GAME

In the 1960s, Robert S. de Ropp, PhD, wrote a book called *The Master Game: Pathways to Higher Consciousness Beyond the Drug Experience* in which he describes two types of life games. I examined his ideas in some detail in the first chapter of my book *Visionseeker: Shared Wisdom from the Place of Refuge*, yet for our purposes here, allow me to add that from his perspective, those who play "the object games"—the fame game, the military game, the money game, for example—do so to master and acquire things of the outer world, such as money, power, sex, and status. Those who play "meta games"—the art game, the science game, the religion game, for example—are interested in mastering and acquiring the intangible things of the inner worlds, such as knowledge, beauty, truth, and the salvation of the soul. At the apex of all the meta games is the "Master Game." The goal of this life game is spiritual awakening, enlightenment, and liberation, through which we may discover our own true nature and the nature of just about everything around us.[2]

Mystics, saints, and shamans—the inspired visionaries within all of the world's cultures—are the original players of the Master Game, exploring and mastering the inner worlds of spirit through the vehicle of their own mind and consciousness. I can tell you from firsthand experience that once you step onto the time-tested path of the shaman, the Master Game quickly becomes the only game worth playing. And the path of the shaman is a time-tested way that can lead us successfully through the seat of initiation that we find ourselves traveling right now.

The Path of the Shaman

Shamans still exist in some form in every culture on the planet, including our own modernized Western world. Engaging with the shamanic tradition is not about cultural appropriation or ripping off the spirituality of any indigenous peoples. We all come from indigenous ancestors if we go back far enough, and they all had great shamans. Thus, the shamanic path is one of our birthrights and the ancestral precursor of all of our spiritual and religious traditions.

In the Western world, when we hear the word *shaman*, many of us think of a costumed tribal person dancing around a fire in the dark, involved in some sort of mysterious ritual, accompanied by drum beats and singing. But inside that costume and ritual there is a woman or a man with a set of very real skills.

All true shamans are distinguished by their ability to achieve visionary states of consciousness in which they can redirect their focused awareness away from everyday physical reality and into the hidden, inner worlds, all while very much awake. This conscious shifting of awareness is called shamanic journeywork in the Western world, and it's an ancient form of meditation that improves with practice. It has been my experience that most of us in the West can do this to some extent, and some of us are real naturals at it. In shamanic journeywork, we quiet ourselves, focus our intentions upon the inner worlds, and watch. Shamanic practice thus begins with intention, and we trust that the rest just happens.

The first thing those with shamanic abilities discover is that the hidden inner worlds are inhabited by transpersonal forces that the traditional peoples call *spirits*—the spirits of nature, the spirits of the elementals, the spirits of our ancestors, the spirits of the dead, as well as higher angelic forces, many of whom serve humanity as helpers and guardians, teachers and guides, and there are others. The imaginary friends many of us had as children most likely fall into one or more of these categories.

It is this extraordinary ability to connect with the inner worlds of things hidden and the beings that reside there that sets shamans apart from all other religious practitioners. I remember asking Michael Harner long ago what qualities revealed someone as an authentic shaman. He replied, "Do they journey to other worlds? Do they have relationships with spirits? And do they perform miracles?" It is through their relationship with the spirits that shamans are able to do various things, initially on behalf of themselves and then increasingly on behalf of others. And of the things shamans can do, many could be said to fall into the realm of the miraculous. What sorts of things are these, you might ask?

EMPOWERMENT

Working with the assistance of their helping spirits, those transpersonal forces with whom they establish relationship, shamans are able to restore power to persons who have been dramatically disempowered and diminished by their life experiences. This is what I experienced when Sandra Ingerman reconnected me with my childhood spirit friend. The rest of my life then began to unfold in an empowered way, and nothing has ever been quite the same.

Recently I had the opportunity to be of service in this way for an old friend from high school who attended a workshop I was offering in Oregon. Mark and I had seen each other only twice in the past fifty years or so, but there was still a heart connection. As part of a demonstration for the group, I invited Mark to volunteer for an empowerment exercise known as a power-animal retrieval, in which I as the giver would attempt to find a spirit helper for him as the receiver. In the process I would ask the spirit to provide him with power, protection, and support. As we lay down on the floor of the workshop room side by side, the other participants watching, Mark was uncertain about what was going on, yet I settled myself beside him and brought my conscious awareness into an inner-world place in the dreaming of nature that I call my sacred garden. I allowed myself to just be there for long moments, then I simply set my intention to invite a helping spirit to reveal itself to me for my friend. My job was simply to watch and to listen.

My attention was drawn to a large tree overhanging a pond. In the tree I saw a good-sized snake, a python or boa, perhaps. I have always been fond of serpents, so I focused my attention upon it and asked the snake, "Are you here for my old friend Mark?" The response came in the form of an emotional pulse—one that I perceived as affection. I took that as a yes. I approached it and gathered the snake into my arms, then transferred my awareness back to the workshop room, holding the serpent in a bundle next to my heart. I then conveyed the snake and its medicine to my friend's heart center with my breath, the way Sandra had done for me so many years earlier.

I didn't know how Mark would respond, as he is a professor of education, very mental. But as I related the journey to him, a funny look came over his face. He then told me that several weeks earlier he had been at the Oregon Country Fair, where he had encountered someone walking around with a large boa draped around himself. This individual then wrapped this big snake around my friend's shoulders. Mark felt the connection with the serpent, and it felt good. He didn't know what to make of it, as he had never been particularly fond of snakes, and when I perceived the serpent in a spiritual relationship with him as a power animal, he was amazed. He now possesses snake medicine, and he will find out through direct experience what that means.

DIVINATION

Shamanic practitioners are able to access information from the inner worlds through divination. I can recall many instances in which I and others have been able to be in service to another person using divination, accessing information or symbols on the person's behalf in response to their request about specific issues. I simply quiet myself, and using a rattle or a drum for liftoff, I access the expanded state of awareness in which I first connect with my own helping spirits and then put out there the questions I have been asked. Then I simply listen and watch. The information that comes through my mind, verbal or symbolic, is sometimes cryptic though invariably on the mark. Accessing information this way is not difficult to do once you learn how. It's simply a matter of practice, and once again, the buzzword is trust.

PSYCHOPOMP

Some shamanic practitioners are good at guiding the souls of the recently deceased to where they are to go in the afterlife, a skill known as psychopomp work. In our Western culture, we have priests of many different varieties who are adept at conducting funerals or celebration-of-life ceremonies, but how many can track the soul of a recently deceased person, connect with it, and guide that soul to where it is supposed to go next on its journey "home"? This ability resides in the realm of the shaman.

I would like to share one of my more recent shamanic dreams that involved psychopomp work, one in which I became aware that I was dreaming and encountered a discarnate soul in need.

I awoke at first light with my lady, Jill, asleep next to me in bed. As I allowed myself to slip back into my dreaming, my vision came up as it often does at this time of day, and I found myself lying on the slope of a hillside under many big trees in full leaf. The imagery became more dense and I sensed the presence of others. Looking up, I saw several children hanging in the air above me on what appeared to be a swing with no ropes. It was simply floating. The children observed me curiously. They seemed to be sitting among garlands of flowers and greenery that were part of the swing seat.

I then became aware that someone had embraced me in a full-body hug. Whoever it was literally wrapped themselves around me like a python, immobilizing me completely. I could barely breathe and could not disengage. As I tried to extricate myself, the person tightened around me like a wrestler who has you in their grip. I felt some alarm and sent a mental probe toward this person. In response, I felt his fear and his deep remorse. I knew in those moments that it was indeed a him, and I also felt his need for reassurance and help.

"Who are you?" I asked. All I sensed was confusion and turmoil, but I did get a response. I was in contact. "Do you need help?" I asked. The coils of his arms and legs that were wrapped around me loosened slightly. I took this as a yes.

Slowly, I felt the grip of this terrified, confused soul begin to relinquish its hold on me. As I felt his release, the shamanic trance state deepened and I felt myself suffused with the familiar ecstatic sensations of overwhelming power or force. My body (in bed) began to shake. I could not control it. I was now completely possessed by this force, and I could only hold on to the emerging whirlwind within and around me and try my best to direct it with my conscious awareness. The power held me immobilized as the soaring ecstasy continued to amp up, and I knew that this meant that the spirits were arriving.

They came in a procession, like a parade, and I could both see them as well as feel them observing me curiously as I lay sprawled, paralyzed, on that hillside under the trees. There, to one side, was the one who needed help. He looked like a stiffened cadaver curled up on his back. I had no idea who he was.

The procession of spirits slowly passed by. They all seemed to be wearing masks, human masks like those worn in the carnival in Venice. I noted that the spirits all seemed to be female. As they passed, I could feel their spirit bodies, the "robes" that were their energetic fields, sweep me gently, pressing curiously against me as if they were offering their support.

In response to each, my body surged again and again with sensations of "the power." I felt one of them pause and run her fingers through my hair, lifting it upward, and words came into my mind—that the power was coming into me through my hair. I thought briefly of the biblical hero Samson and felt the spirit's amusement.

I glanced over at the one in need, and it came to me that he wanted to die, that he wanted to kill himself, and with this insight I realized that he already had. I knew that he (his soul) was in a personal hell realm of his own postmortem dreaming and that he was suffering and afraid. I understood that he needed to cross over into the transitional world between life and the afterlife. As I tried to engage him again and tell him this, a curious impulse emerged in my ecstasy-drugged mind, and I knew that before he could cross over, he needed to tell his story. He had to do this so that he would not be forgotten, so that he would be remembered for who he once was.

I extended my awareness toward him and said, "You need to tell me your story. And then you will be free." There was hesitation, and then I could feel him begin to coil around me again as his fear gripped him. Suddenly, I began to receive the story of his life. I got it in spurts, each one representing a vignette, and then in an instant, I received the transmission of all of it in one long download, all of his loneliness and pain and sorrow, his few successes and his many failures, a very strange and sad tale. After his sharing, I felt him relax.

At this point a very unusual message appeared in my mind. I offer it here without understanding what it means. He said, "Bury me standing because I spent my whole life on my knees." The impact of this statement shook me, so I said to him, "Now you are free, and you will not be forgotten." Reassured, he relinquished his grip on me.

In that space, I perceived another spirit who detached herself from the procession passing by. She stood over me, and I could see her eyes looking down through her human mask.

I observed her completely and caught glimpses of her sensuous belly briefly revealed by her swirling blue and white robes. She moved forward, slowly enfolding and embracing me, her salty lips suddenly brushing mine. And then she was kissing me.

It was *her*—the queen of the sea, the mother, the orisha that the Yorubas call Yemoja, Brazilians call Iemanja, Cubans call Yemaya, Vodou practitioners call La Sirene, Hawaiians call Namakaokahai. It was the water woman, the one who had been following me all these years since my first contact with her fifty years ago in West Africa, the one who often comes to assist me at my healing ceremonies for those in need.

The procession continued to pass by as she held me in her embrace, kissing me more and more ardently. I managed to surface as my sensual side emerged. Still gripped by my trance, I was aware that I was still in bed next to my wife.

With this thought, I whispered against the water spirit's mouth, "You are being very naughty."

She giggled with the delight of it, and I felt her hands stroking my ecstasy-gripped soul and my body as well.

"Will you help with that one?" I asked, indicating the tortured soul who was still curled up nearby.

"Of course," she whispered against my mouth. "It is done."

And in an instant, he was gone, conveyed across to where he was supposed to go in the afterlife, his trials over.

Slowly, her mouth disengaged from mine and her arms released me. In response, the shamanic trance diminished in surges, each pulse of power less than the last.

I sensed rather than heard her words of farewell, and I felt the love that she held for me, and I for her.

The physical paralysis lessened as the shamanic dream faded, and my awareness slowly transferred back to my body lying in bed next to Jill. She was holding me in her sleep, and I felt the great love that we share with each other, the love of the gods, expressed and experienced through us here.

I slowly reviewed the dream, again and again, and at the end, a sound appeared in my mind's ear, a sound like wind chimes tinkling, the laughter of the saltwater oceanic goddess suffused with her delight. Then I emerged fully, disengaged gently from Jill's embrace without waking her, and taking a pad of paper and pen I wrote down what had just occurred.

Weather Working

Some shamanic practitioners are adept at working with the weather, and this is without a doubt an ancient practice developed and refined across time. Here is an example.

On a Saturday afternoon in March 2010, just after the release of *Awakening to the Spirit World: The Shamanic Path of Direct Revelation*, my book co-authored with Sandra Ingerman, I had scheduled a book signing followed by a mini workshop at a local bookstore called Kona Stories here on the island of Hawai'i. Jill was with me, and we were discussing what we might do with the workshop group, drawing upon the book to bring forth some of its shared wisdom.

Both of us were much aware that our district on Hawai'i Island had been in a severe drought for several years, and the land and trees were in dire need of water. Accordingly, we decided to draw on the chapter in *Awakening* that deals with working with the weather and environmental changes. The workshop group convened, and after a short discussion about modern shamans and the nature of their practice, I gave a brief overview of meditative shamanic journeywork and how it works. I then asked if they would like to engage in some weather work, specifically to attract rain. Everyone liked this idea.

I got out my drum. We suggested that at the journey's beginning each of the participants listen to the drum either while sitting or lying down with eyes closed. Each of us would then transfer our awareness (journey) to a place on the island where we felt connected, a personal place where we felt at ease and empowered. Once there, each was to settle and make a prayer to the great Hawaiian deity Lono, the transpersonal force associated with agriculture, healing, navigation, and science. Lono is also the keeper of the winds and the bringer of rain, and so each of us would humbly ask this spirit to bring forth rain to nurture our dry island.

The participants were to perceive themselves sitting in meditation in that place on the island and "to remember rain." This meant that each was to visualize the clouds gathering above this place, to smell the moisture building in the air, to feel the wind coming and the first fine drops on their skin, and to hear the force of the rain coming through the trees. Finally, we were to experience ourselves in the midst of the rain as it pummeled down, drenching and sustaining the land with the water of life.

That was it. We held the journey constant with the drum for twenty minutes or so then brought everyone back. We discussed what we had perceived, sharing our journeys with each other, and then we dispersed, confident that with our having made rain magic, Lono would respond.

Some participants got a sprinkle where they lived that very evening, and within a day the island received a deep, driving tropical rain, the gutters on our roof edges overflowing as Lono responded to our prayer. Many e-mailed us with wonder, even from neighboring islands. The television weather commentators were amazed, as they simply hadn't seen this storm coming. It just appeared over our island.

In sharing this with you, the reader, allow me to acknowledge that this was not about me flexing my spiritual muscle. This ritual was about *we,* about all of us in that circle working in connection, engaging the spirits, singing their praises, and sharing our needs. We did this ritual with a common focus and intention, and with the assistance and support of the deity Lono, the land and our souls were refreshed, the drought ended, and the rainy season began early that year.

This story also reveals a shamanic truth: when the transpersonal forces that we call spirits are engaged, and when "the field" is favorable, there can be a response. The why of it is elusive; this is part of the Mystery that we cannot really know.

Yet when we are paying attention and coming from a place of compassionate intention for the greater good, things do have the tendency to happen.

Hunting Magic

Traditionally, shamans served their communities as the mediators between the human world and the world of nature, the source of food and all good things upon which the community depended for their continued survival. Rock shelters and cave sites have preserved pictographs and petroglyphs that reveal the shaman's connection with the spirits of the animals that were hunted by the people—spirits with whom the shaman had to maintain a good working relationship. If the shaman failed to maintain this balance, the people might starve.

Imagine that you are an American Indian, perhaps a Hopi or a Zuni, living in one of the pueblos on top of one of the mesas three hundred years ago in what is today the American Southwest. Imagine that it is spring and that the life is returning to the land. The corn has been planted, and it is growing, though it has not yet borne fruit. The winter has been hard. The piki bread made from last year's corn has been consumed. The people are starving. The children are crying, for there is no milk in their mothers' breasts. It is time for the men to hunt.

In accordance with ancient custom, the men withdraw into the kiva, the community sacred room built down into the ground. It is time for ceremony, and the shamans will likely lead those ceremonies. Perhaps they approach the large pot where the sacred fetishes of the animal spirits are kept and periodically fed with cornmeal. Perhaps the animal first addressed is mountain lion. Its fetish is withdrawn from the pot and becomes the focus of the ritual, for in addition to being the guardian of the north, mountain lion is also the elder brother of all the animals. His permission to hunt is required, and his support for the endeavor is necessary for a successful outcome.

Next, the spirit of deer, the elder brother of all deer, is addressed. It is deer that the hunters wish to hunt, yet protocol is everything. The shamans go into a trance and journey into the spirit worlds to connect with sacred brother deer, the oversoul of all deer, and make their plea: "The people are starving. The children are crying. We, the people, need you to send some of your deer people out of the mountains, down to the hunters' bows. And when we kill them, we will let their souls out of their skins. And we will invite their souls to come back to the pueblo with us so that as we eat their meat, we can celebrate their souls and your spirit. There will be singing and dancing and music."

The shaman understands that the deer oversoul includes within itself all of the deer souls who manifest into our world as deer. The shaman also knows that the animal and plant spirits love music. When the pueblo people plant corn, they always sing. It doesn't matter what they sing. What matters is that they do it. The corn maiden hears the music, and the corn grows and offers many ears in response. The deer spirit loves music too.

The shaman prevails, and a bargain is made. The deer spirit will send four deer people to the hunters, who must wait for them at such and such a place. The shaman advises the hunters, who then do more ceremony before they go to that place and wait. The deer arrive and allow themselves to be sacrificed to feed the starving humans. Their souls follow the humans back to the pueblo, where their meat is cooked, and the people offer their gratitude through singing and music and ritual.

The deer souls are now released. They return to where the deer oversoul resides in the spirit worlds and dreams. As they resume residence within the spiritual field of deer, all the other deer spirits therein are curious. The incomers tell them what has occurred, that they allowed the humans to kill them and let their souls out of their skins, and that they went back to the pueblo with the humans where they were celebrated with singing and dancing and music.

The other deer spirits are very interested in this, and they say, "Music? We love music. Maybe we'll let the hunters kill us too so that we can have this wonderful experience."

Hunting magic is still performed by indigenous peoples living in close proximity to nature. Today, most of us in the Western world buy our food at the supermarket, yet we can still employ a form of hunting magic. Whenever I prepare food, I always pause to acknowledge the source of the meat or fish or corn or squash and offer my gratitude. It is my hope that the hunters and fishermen among us engage in some sort of ritual before they practice their craft. Whenever I cut a stalk of bananas from our groves on our family farm on Hawai'i Island, I remember that the bananas and I share forty percent of our DNA in common. So during those moments, machete in hand, I offer those banana trees my profound respect and gratitude for providing my family and me with sustenance. And whenever Jill and I plant or harvest other food crops on our land in south Kona, she always consults the Hawaiian moon calendar for fishing and farming, and I always sing. It doesn't matter how you offer gratitude and respect; what matters is that you do it.

HEALING

Shamans may also be master healers at the physical, mental-emotional, and spiritual levels of being. In their role as healers, many practitioners of shamanism are accomplished at restoring the fabric of a client's soul, a transpersonal healing modality known as soul retrieval. As discussed by Jill in our co-authored book *Spirit Medicine: Healing in the Sacred Realms*, soul loss happens when parts of the soul complex (to be discussed shortly) become dissociated, often in response to severe trauma. In the indigenous perspective, this dissociation is one of the classic causes of illness and premature death, yet curiously, soul loss is not even mentioned in our Western medical textbooks. Nor are Jill's insights into the transpersonal healing modality known as soul retrieval mentioned therein.

Sanctified by their initiatory experiences and accompanied by their spirit guardians, shamans alone among human beings are able to expand their conscious awareness and travel into the spiritual worlds to recover those dissociated soul parts, returning them to their original owners with the assistance of their helping spirits, thus restoring and renewing the matrix of their client's soul. Not surprisingly, many recipients of soul retrieval describe their responses to this experience as life changing.

Jill has performed more than four thousand soul retrieval rituals on behalf of her clients over the past twenty years. We have often shared the following account in our teaching workshops, a story of how Jill was able to be of service in a long-distance soul retrieval for a man we'll call Bob.

We lived in California at that time, and a woman friend of Jill's had just attended her high school reunion in Minneapolis. There she encountered Bob, her high school sweetie. Upon graduation, she and Bob had gone their separate ways, had careers and families and children, and now were both widowed, their children grown and gone. Upon meeting once again at the reunion, they discovered that the spark of love and attraction was still there.

Despite the spark, Bob felt he was unable to commit to another long-term relationship because of something that had happened to him as a boy, something that had profoundly wounded him emotionally, leaving him rather remote at that level. He was in

Catholic parochial school at that time, and when he was in third grade, on the first day of the new school year, his class was going to have the ritual of Holy Communion in the front of the chapel before any of the other grades. This was an initiation, and he was really, really looking forward to it.

When he got to school on that day, he was thirsty and ran to drink from a water fountain only to feel an iron fist gripping his neck from behind and hauling him upright. It was one of the nuns informing him point blank that he had been told not to eat or drink before coming to school and taking part in communion. "No communion for you!" she proclaimed with grim finality. Eight-year-old Bob then had to sit alone in the front of the chapel while his entire class got up to have communion. On that day, he had experienced a profound and enduring soul loss. In fact, he could not speak of this event for thirty years, nor could he relate it without crying for forty.

Jill's friend told Bob about her work in soul retrieval, and he wondered if she might be able to help him. Bob connected with Jill by phone, and she agreed to do a long-distance soul retrieval for him. She would go to her office, she told him, where she would state her intentions for him. She would then expand her conscious awareness into the shamanic state and connect with her spirits, who would advise her and help her journey to recover his lost soul part. She would then send this soul part back to him while he was sitting in a park (a place in nature) in Minneapolis.

At the day and time agreed upon, Jill did just that, and when her inner vision came up, she found herself with her team of spirit helpers in the back of a church. The building was empty, yet Jill intuited that this was the church where the soul loss had transpired. In vision, she and her team walked down the central aisle, and way up in the front pew she could see a tiny head. When she turned the corner, she saw a little boy sitting there.

He appeared to be made of stone, of marble, frozen. It was Bob's eight-year-old soul part, still waiting for communion.

As she quietly observed him, an intuitive download appeared in her mind, and she asked the powers at large if there was any other spirit who would like to come forward to be of service to Bob at this time. Immediately, a door opened in the back of the church and a luminous form entered and floated down the side aisle. On turning the corner, the spirit took the shape of a tall bearded man with long hair who was wrapped in robes made of light. He was smiling with radiant benevolence, and in that moment Jill felt that it could well be the spirit of Jesus of Nazareth himself.

She explained to the spirit why she was there and told him the story of Bob, the frozen stone boy sitting before them. The revered healer turned his attention upon the boy for long, thoughtful moments, and then leaning over, he breathed into his face. Two pink spots appeared in the boy's cheeks. With successive breaths, again and again, the spirit blew life force back into the small figure who slowly thawed, becoming a living boy once again.

Little Bob sat blinking up at Jill and the tall spirit beside her, and as Jill prepared to gather him into her arms, she became aware that the spirit had withdrawn into the front of the church. When she turned, she saw the spirit come back, bearing the tray with the wafers and the wine, whereupon he served that little boy communion.

When the ceremony was complete, the spirit, with a smile, slowly dissolved into a misty cloud that simply disappeared, leaving an impression within Jill that she would never forget. She then gathered the boy into her arms and transferred her conscious awareness back to her office in California where she intentionally used her own breath to blow Bob's soul part back into him as he was sitting in the park in Minneapolis, and then recorded the entire episode on a compact disc and sent it to him Priority Mail.

In response to his soul's renewal, Bob recovered his emotional strength and proposed to his high school sweetie. They married and lived happily ever after until his passing more than a dozen years later.

In discussing shamanic healing, it is worth noting that while every shaman is a medicine person, not all medicine people are shamans. Like shamans, medicine people often function as ceremonialists and ritual leaders, working on behalf of large numbers of people, even entire communities at once. Yet most of the medicine people that I have encountered in both the indigenous and Western worlds are not shamans, but rather fulfill social roles more like those of priests or priestesses.

Like shamans, medicine people may hold considerable understanding of physical medicine and perform tasks such as mending broken bones, healing wounds, preventing infections, facilitating childbirth, and treating illnesses with their knowledge of herbs and medicinal plants and through other healing modalities, including energy work. However, medicine people tend to do their main work in the objective, physical reality of things seen. All our specialists in modern Western medicine—our physicians and surgeons, our naturopaths and homeopaths, our energy workers and acupuncturists, our midwives and many practitioners in our psychotherapeutic communities who are in service through the medium of talk therapy—are medicine people.

By contrast, shamans do their main work in the spirit worlds in states of deep trance. Many do not engage in lengthy ceremonies, although some do. In such cases, they do what is necessary to create a sacred space and expand their conscious awareness. They then work in tandem with their helping spirits in the transpersonal levels of reality to accomplish what needs to be done. Shamans are medicine people who know that all illnesses have a spiritual aspect, and by working with their helping spirits to diminish the spiritual aspect of an illness, they may diminish, even eliminate, its expression into our physical world of form.

An authentic shaman's work with spirits is not the same as straight-on energy work, although it does involve energy. Shamans use their own bodies and minds to create bridges between the personal world of form and the transpersonal worlds of the spirits. And when that bridge is formed and the spirits are engaged, it allows the healing and harmonizing powers of the spirits to flow across that bridge and into our world to manifest something—healing, for example. I should also note that some healing practitioners function as shamans, as energy workers, and as ceremonial leaders as the need exists. And most indigenous shamans also know a great deal about physical medicine.

Shamanic State of Consciousness and the Technology of Transcendence

In my work as an anthropologist and because of my books about my own experiences on the shaman's path, I have been brought into close connection with increasing numbers of modern spiritual seekers at conferences and workshops over the past thirty years. I have watched, riveted, as nontribal Westerners successfully achieve shamanic states of trance, often on the very first attempt, and I've listened to their stories of their inner adventures recounted upon their return—accounts that would pass muster at any Aboriginal campfire. It may be that tens of millions of people—maybe more—have these abilities.

Evidence from my own experiential workshops has led me and others to suspect that there may be a biological-energetic program on our DNA—on our genetic hard drive, so to speak—and when this program is double-clicked with the right mouse, higher functions coded into the personal mind-body matrix may be awakened.

In response, our consciousness may expand dramatically, allowing us to have that direct, mystical connection with the sacred realms that defines the shaman. I believe now that this is what happened for me on the clay pan in Ethiopia so many years ago.

The inner fieldwork of the Eastern mystics suggests that this biological-energetic program is associated with the ductless glands, the brain, and the heart—organs that, in turn, are in relationship with those dense concentrations of energy known in the East as chakras and are located in the core of our personal etheric matrix. When these physical and energetic mission-control centers are activated, the relationship between them can dramatically affect the body and the brain, which may undergo striking changes as a result.

It is also known that the people in indigenous societies have developed techniques for altering consciousness in specific ways. These techniques constitute a form of technology—a technology of transcendence.

When I was living among indigenous traditional people in Africa, I learned that they know everything there is to know about their surrounding environments. If there are psychotropic plants growing nearby, the ritual use of hallucinogens derived from these plant teachers is sometimes utilized to expand consciousness and access the inner, hidden realms. This type of visioning is always carried out in ceremonial circumstances steeped in cultural significance.

The visionary explorers Terence McKenna, Ralph Metzner, and Michael Harner are among many who have revealed that the same use of hallucinogens held true for the mystery schools in the ancient world. The growing literature on hallucinogens reveals striking cross-cultural similarities in the reported effects of these natural substances on human consciousness. These effects include the capacity to channel the energy of the universe, to discover the most profound secrets of nature, and to acquire wisdom that may be used for magical, medical, and religious purposes. But taking a hallucinogen and seeing visions does not necessarily make someone a shaman.

Equally powerful and far more widespread are the psychological and physiological methods that the shamans of the traditional peoples have developed for altering consciousness and repatterning it in specific ways—techniques such as fasting and sleep deprivation, physical exhaustion and hyperventilation, and subjecting the body to temperature extremes during rituals of purification, such as the sweat lodge.

It is also generally known that the intensely physical stimulus of monotonous drumming and rattling, combined with culturally meaningful ritual and ceremony, prayer and chant, singing and dancing, can be equally effective in shifting consciousness into visionary modes of perception. Not surprisingly, the use of drums and rattles by shamanic practitioners around the world is almost universal. Shifting consciousness by means of the drum and rattle is the time-tested method that Jill and I use in our training workshops.

Until relatively recently, most Westerners have tended to regard the whole issue of altered-state experiences as mysterious, paranormal, or even pathological, and so some, in ignorance, still fear and reject the idea of expanded awareness and connection with helping spirits and guides. By contrast, in a traditional indigenous society, each child grows up with elder ceremonial leaders and shamans who are able to access expanded states of consciousness intentionally for the benefit of themselves, for others, and for the entire community. They know that virtually everyone can learn how to access sacred states of consciousness to some extent. They also know that some of us are real naturals at it.

The shamanic state of consciousness can now be partially understood in scientific terms. It is known, for example, that the nature and quality of the visionary experience can be determined to some extent by our focused intentionality, by our belief systems, and by the setting in which we find ourselves. These may serve as patterning forces that can reshape our visionary experience once our initial state of consciousness has been destabilized by the drum, the rattle, or the hallucinogen, if one was used.

With more than thirty years of apprenticeship in this tradition, I have learned that the achieving of this expanded state of consciousness is a learned skill that improves with practice—a skill that can give seekers access to many varieties of experience, including connection with the spirit world, if that is their intention. Experience with an indigenous spiritual tradition and cultural overlay is often useful and interesting, but it is not required (although some feel it is).

I also know with absolute certainty that the program, once activated, allows us to ascend toward the luminous horizon of our personal and collective destiny in a completely new way. Traditional people would agree with this statement because they know a great secret: any human activity or endeavor can be enormously enhanced through utilizing and eventually mastering this sacred technology.

The Path of the Modern Shaman

The shaman's path emerges from the seat of initiation as part of the cultural heritage of all people everywhere. As I have said, it is one of our birthrights, although it was largely lost in the West due to ruthless and barbarous suppression by Christianity during the Middle Ages.

Interestingly, shamanism is not a religion, nor does it conflict with any religious tradition. As Michael Harner has affirmed, it is a method for exploring the connections between humanity and all of creation. And when this method is practiced with humility, reverence, and self-discipline, the shaman's visionary path can become a way of life, one that may enrich our everyday experience beyond measure, as well as contribute to raising and expanding the consciousness of humankind. From my perspective as an anthropologist who has spent large parts of my life living with traditional indigenous peoples, shamanism is our key to a re-enchantment of the world and a re-enchantment of ourselves.

As we experience the ending of one cycle of ages and the beginning of the next, a growing number of accomplished teachers and practitioners in the Western world are creating a modern upgrade of the ancient path of the shaman. A new shamanic tradition has taken form over the past forty years, one that could be called Western shamanism. This new form of shamanism reflects who we are now, as well as who we are becoming.

Because this is a new form of shamanism, it seems fitting that there be a new term for those who practice it. Why? Because those who practice shamanism usually do not claim to be shamans. Authentic shamans tend to be very humble people. Calling themselves shamans just isn't done, because doing so is regarded as spiritual arrogance and a quick way to lose one's power. True shamans are aware that the power to which they have access—the power that enables them to facilitate healing, for example—is not theirs to claim. Rather, it is the power of the universe, on loan and channeled through the spirits who work with them. The term *shaman* is thus an appellation that can only be given to them by the spirits and by the members of their communities, based on their abilities to be of service.

Those who practice Buddhism do not claim to be Buddhas; they call themselves Buddhists. Those who practice Taoism call themselves Taoists. In this same vein, perhaps those of us following the shamanic path today could call ourselves *shamanists*.

Whatever we are called, we know that by utilizing the shamans' time-tested methodology, we can awaken from the consensual slumber of culture at large, and it then becomes possible to personally experience a reunion—one of unlimited power and connection—with a mysterious, godlike mind. We then know with certainty that no holy words or books, no secret ceremonies or rituals, and no spiritual leaders or gurus or faiths can convey these experiences to us. This is why the shaman's path is, and has always been, one of direct revelation. Once the higher evolutionary functions are triggered within us, some mysterious, predetermined schedule is set into motion, activating a program that cannot be given to us by any outside agency.

This is because most of us already have it.

Sophia's Dream

Science has revealed conclusively that despite the well-funded efforts of the climate deniers, the big climatic shift is already upon us, one that will utterly change our world, our societies, and our lives. This means that the decisions we make in the here and now will create a foundation that will affect the lives and spiritual practices of all of humanity for the next several generations, perhaps the next thousand years, and this is not a small thing.

My great Hawaiian friend, the kahuna Hale Makua, often observed that the foundation stone for Indigenous Mind is respect. By contrast, the foundation for Western Mind is dominion. Our Judeo-Christian mythos gave us human domination over the natural world and each other, and this mode of operating is simply not sustainable.

In my humble opinion, the time has come for an upgrade in our cultural mythos, and at all levels, one that will include respect for that which will serve and support us forever. I'm talking about nature, and forever is a very long time. I have come to suspect that the experience of our re-enchantment may hold the guarantee of humanity's continued survival on planet Earth, as well as a guarantee of our thriving during the centuries and the millennia to come. This is because modern visionaries hold profound and enduring reverence for everyone and everything that we encounter in life—and for the All-That-Is. In a mythic sense, this All-That-Is is none other than Mother Nature, the world soul called Sophia (pronounced So-FAI-yah) by the Gnostics.

SOPHIA

In 2010, Michael Craft, who worked in the programming department at the Omega Institute in Rhinebeck, New York, gave me the book *Not in His Image: Gnostic Vision, Sacred Ecology, and the Future of Belief* by a metahistorian named John Lamb Lash. In it, Lash reveals that the mystery schools of the ancient world proclaimed Sophia, the soul of our world, to be an immensely wise, sentient being. They also held that the physical embodiment of Sophia is our beautiful planet Earth, which many today refer to as Gaia, following the teachings of the ancient Greeks and the ideas of the scientist and visionary James Lovelock. The Gnostics of the classical period described Sophia's spiritual essence as a visible milky white light with a voice and vast intelligence.[1]

We're talking about that organic, misty radiance that possesses a godlike mind. Visionaries and mystics across time have achieved communion with this intelligence, and it may impart knowledge and guidance directly to us, if we are so honored.

Do you remember the story of the biblical prophet Elijah finding himself in the presence of an angel of the Lord in the ninth century BCE? He didn't see this being as a winged super-human. He saw it as a white light, a brilliant radiance with a voice. That's Sophia.

In a mythic perspective, Sophia was, is, and will forever be the great planetary mother goddess of which all other earthbound goddesses are aspects. Sophia is the authentic transpersonal force that infuses everything on our beautiful world, including ourselves, with life. Her fierce yet compassionate being is like a river of energy that flows within and through everything, and having a direct experience of this energy may transform us utterly, just as it did the prophets and mystics of the ancient world. It is available to all of us and all the time, because no matter what our religious beliefs may be, the fact that we all inhabit physical bodies derived from planet Earth means that we are all her children—all of us. We are all manifested aspects of her.

I myself was honored to encounter Sophia at the bottom of a cinder crater on the side of the great mountain of vision Mauna Kea on Hawai'i Island in 2003, a story I share in *The Bowl of Light*. It was under the guidance of the kahuna Hale Makua that she appeared to me in a spirit vision as a mass of living white light with a voice. To say I was impressed would be an understatement of vast proportions. I was stunned.

Years later, after reading Lash's book, I connected with Lash himself through his website. In our third or fourth e-mail exchange, he revealed that he had established an ongoing mystical connection with Sophia and that he had even given her a new name to which she seemed to respond. Allow me to note here that the soul of our world inhabits the living biosphere of our planet—and more. Lash revealed further that Sophia likes diversity and innovation, and in his sharing of this new name with me, I decided to try it out to see if she would respond to me.

I live in the district of south Kona of Hawai'i Island, and so on a bright sunny morning I went down to the coast. The immense ocean stretching to the horizon was flat, virtually no waves. I walked right to the end of a black lava flow at the edge of the sparkling blue water. I watched the ocean surging back and forth for a while, then closed my eyes and accessed the shamanic state of consciousness, expanding my awareness. I waited for perhaps five minutes, allowing myself to settle, before I turned my attention toward Sophia and uttered her new name, the one that Lash had given me. I said it three times in a breathy whisper as though I was talking to my lover while holding her in my arms during a joyous marital encounter.

I held the state . . . held the state . . . and then slowly opened my eyes. There before me, the flat dark ocean remained for long moments. Suddenly, it swelled into a large wave that rolled in and almost burst upon me but stopped right at my feet. Again, and then once more—two more large waves in succession rushed in and stopped right at my feet, three waves in all. The ocean then flattened out and was calm once again. I took that as a response.

Not long after, I found myself at the Breitenbush Conference Center in northern Oregon where I offer workshops several times each year. It was late July in 2010 and it was very hot. I parked in the lot and then walked down a long road through the shade of a forest of great conifers more than a hundred feet high and headed for the office to check in. The forest was hushed in the breathless heat. As I walked, I remembered the waves.

I stopped. I looked around. I was alone on the road. On impulse I closed my eyes. With a few clearing breaths, I accessed the shamanic state. As before, I focused my attention toward Sophia and uttered her name, the one Lash shared with me. I whispered it three times and then waited. For a while, nothing . . . and then a wind came rushing up the road toward me through that tunnel of trees. In seconds I was surrounded by a swirling vortex of cold air that engulfed me, throwing up dust and blowing my hair back from my face. And I mean cold. I took this as a response. And then the wind simply vanished, leaving me with great gratitude welling in my heart. A chortling croak from above revealed a large raven watching me with a flat stare. I croaked back. It is at moments like this that I know with absolute certainty that magic is real.

In sharing these narratives with you, I am revealing what is possible for those of us who choose to walk the visionary path. And should you decide to extend your aloha toward Sophia, you can create your own name that you may offer to her with your love. And love seems to be the key. You can do something as simple as I did, or you could do ceremony in whatever way seems appropriate. It doesn't matter what ceremony you do or how you do it. What matters is that you do it and do it with love. With your continued practice, Sophia will respond, for as Lash revealed, the soul of this world rejoices in novelty and diversity, a universal impulse perhaps that she, as a creator being, brought in with her from the pleroma, the center of our galaxy.

THE ORIGINATOR

In *Not in His Image*, Lash tells us that the mystery schools of the past held that Sophia emerged in the remote past from our galactic core (the pleroma), from which she streamed out into the arms of chaos (the kenoma). She did not emerge as an angelic humanoid, but rather as a river of conscious light. She is one of the Aeons (EYE-ons)—immortal, archetypal, Dreamtime creator beings who reside within the galactic core and who are emanations and aspects of the mysterious Source that the Gnostics called the Originator.[2]

Many have attempted to describe the Originator in different ways across time. I myself have made an attempt. The following words, first recorded in *Visionseeker*, came to me in a Quaker meeting house in Nashville, Tennessee, as I sought to translate my own percepts of the Originator into concepts:

> There is no room
> for set decrees
> or specific laws
> in a sea of grace
> that knows no boundaries
> and has no shores.[3]

Although some are inclined to label the Originator as "God" and worship it, in my experience it is not a being with which we as humans can interact, nor does it respond to or receive worship. It simply exists as an extraordinary dimensional level of reality, perhaps the primary one. As such, it remains utterly remote, fathomless, and unapproachable, and despite all good intentions, it will not receive or respond to our prayers.

Some call it the Source. Others call it Tao, and master Lao-Tzu (in the *Tao Te Ching*) proclaims that the Tao that can be described is not the true Tao. Despite this, I have come to think of it as a limitless, timeless field of living light loaded with potential and its own infinite intelligence. Some mystics have called it the Great Central Sun, and as such, it just is. Makua called the Source by its Tahitian name, Teave (Tay-YA-vey)—tea, meaning "glowing orb," "flame," "source of light," or "progenitor," and *Ve*—"the one who sees all."

It is not "the Creator," by the way. From my direct experience of it, the Source does not create; it emanates, and it does so all the time, whatever time is at its level. Once it emanates parts of itself outward, those parts become dual, and a different dimensional level of reality comes into being inhabited by a dual-natured force—the masculine and feminine forces of creation through which everything else is manifested. Hale Makua confirmed this in *The Bowl of Light*. Yet at this "lower" dimensional level, there are really three players—the masculine force, the feminine force, and the awareness (consciousness) that each has of the other. This reveals the great secret—that consciousness pre-exists matter.

All manifested phenomena, both objective and subjective, are ultimately emanations of the Originator, brought into being through the dual-natured, masculine-feminine creative principle. This reveals that as the Gnostics and Hale Makua have proclaimed, the Originator is present in everything everywhere. The great Aeons are aspects of it, and they are also creator beings. My own direct experience through shamanic journeywork reveals that the so-called black holes located at the center of each galaxy may be portals into and out of the Originator.[4]

My inner scientist has had to accept that this revelation is simply an aspect of the Mystery that is not knowable but can be experienced directly under the right circumstances. I also have come to accept that it is the nature of the Mystery to remain elusive, to position itself just out there before us, around us, and within us, unreachable and yet always and forever exuding a drawing power, attracting us forward toward that which we are destined to become. Perhaps this attractor pattern is an aspect of the Originator so that all of its parts, emanated outward, will come to know who and what they are and ultimately find their way home.

It is important to be aware that science will not be able to confirm these insights with instrumental verification because science, including physics and its theories of general relativity and quantum mechanics, deals with objective physical reality, whereas the Originator exists on a completely different dimensional level. According to Stephen Hawking in his book *A Brief*

History of Time, our galaxy is only one of some hundred thousand million galaxies, and each contains that many stars or more.[5] This reveals the unimaginable immensity of the universes and puts humanity into perspective in our unimaginable smallness with the Originator as an animating force that inhabits all manifested phenomena.

SOPHIA AND THE DREAMTIME

According to Lash's reworking of Sophia's myth, he reveals that Sophia is actually the one who dreamed us—the Anthropos—and our beautiful world (Earth) into existence. As one of the Aeons, Sophia creates through her dreaming—the same spiritual process that the Australian Aborigines call the Dreamtime. This dreaming is not a creationist concept based upon a mythic fatherly mono-god who lives off-planet and works in mysterious ways. It is a mystical percept based upon direct experience (gnosis) of nature (the great Sophia), which is always and forever true.[6] Her myth reveals the story and the impulse. The scientific fields of evolutionary and molecular biology, paleontology, and chemistry reveal how the dreamings' expression into creation happened.

Understanding the relationship between science and the Dreamtime allows us to know the absolute truth that all of reality—including all of us, our souls and our consciousness, our animal and plant colleagues, and the elemental forces of earth, stone, water, fire, nature, and air—are actually aspects of the Originator, the One, the only true unitive level of reality, awareness, and experience. And yet from my personal discussions with Makua, it is true that the One is also experienced as the Many—that it is immanent while also transcendent, existing within every moment and at every level of reality, from amoebas and worms to eagles and human beings, from oceans and rivers and rocks and mountains to planets and stars, galaxies and universes.

THE MANIFESTO

As I have said, Sophia *is* Mother Nature, the life-giving and life-supporting transpersonal force who is and will always be this world's soul. She is the one who gives us everything she's got and never asks for anything in return. Since each of us resides in a body that is a manifestation of nature, each of us at the physical level is an expression of her dreaming. So when we abuse nature or when we abuse each other, we abuse the world soul.

With the systematic destruction of the great mystery schools of antiquity and the genocide inflicted upon the Gnostics by the early Christians seventeen hundred years ago, the knowledge of the functional place of humanity within the extraordinary dynamic of the world soul was suppressed and then forgotten. The world soul, as well as nature herself, was progressively demonized by the salvationist ideology and redeemer complex of emerging Christianity. The infliction of this ideology upon the European populations of pagan peoples was backed by the might of the Roman military machine as a direct result of the emperor Constantine's conversion to Christianity in the fourth century. Invasive Christian missionary activity became a worldwide phenomenon, and we have been dealing with the aftershocks of this enforced religious complex for seventeen hundred years.

Any well-informed overview of the past reveals the extent to which we have strayed from Sophia's dreaming of who and what we humans are destined to become. It could be observed that we have fallen from our original state of grace into deep error through our greed, denial, ongoing preoccupation with power and money, and unrestrained growth and development, not to mention the distraction of our new gadgets. Whether or not our erroneous behaviors can be reversed and rectified remains to be seen.

The indigenous peoples know that nature does not make compromises, nor does she have the slightest interest in the corporate businessmen's profit margins, the religious zealots' extremist belief systems, the politicians' power agendas, or the lobbyists' special interest groups. Nature doesn't negotiate; she responds, and Sophia appears to be responding to the disharmony in our human sphere. It is possible that the climatic shift already upon us reveals that our politicians and developers, our bankers and lawyers, our corporate and religious elite—they must now rethink their priorities and very quickly.

A manifesto published by James Hansen et al., in the prestigious *Proceedings of the National Academy of Sciences*, reveals that if we continue to do business as usual, the continued existence of the human species (*Homo sapiens*) on this beautiful planet may become untenable.[7] This document was signed by more than fifteen hundred of the world's top scientists. This is science, folks, and it doesn't require that you believe in it. Science deals with facts, not belief systems. Science is.

This manifesto has been recently updated by Hansen et al. in 2016.[8] This alarming paper reveals that sea level rise could be up to five meters (twenty feet) higher than it is today, possibly nine meters (thirty-six feet) by the latter part of this century unless greenhouse gases are radically slashed. This will inundate and subsume most of the world's coastal cities, including London, New York, Los Angeles, San Francisco, Portland, Seattle, San Diego, Miami, Shanghai, Mumbai, Amsterdam, Honolulu, Lagos, and others. Hansen reveals that more than half the world's cities are at risk, and the economic cost of continuing "business as usual" is incalculable, resulting in hundreds of millions of climate refugees. Under these conditions, Hansen and his colleagues suggest it is likely that global governance will completely break down. The evidence is in: the climatic shift is already upon us, and the results will be dire. Our beautiful world will rebalance itself. It always has and it always will. The real question for all of us is, can we save ourselves? Humanity is on the endangered species list.

Because we have ignored and denied the environmental handwriting on the wall over the past thirty years, we have now gone past the point of no return, and we literally have no other strategy but to adapt to the coming changes. And they will be drastic. From my perspective as a scientist whose research specialty involves the study of paleoclimates and evolution, I suspect that Sophia is returning to her equilibrium state in which she has resided for millions of years with no ice at the poles—a greenhouse world in which the life force may proliferate undeterred and the sea level may rise to more than one hundred meters (390 feet) higher than it is today. Sophia seems to be rebalancing herself, as she always has. The question is, will humanity, too, be able to rebalance itself?

THE EVOLUTION OF RELIGION

Evidence from archeology, history, cultural anthropology, and mythology suggests that all of our religious beliefs rest upon a foundation of spiritual encounters that were experienced by powerful, charismatic prophets in the remote past. These prophets were shamans in every sense, and like shamans everywhere, they communicated what they had seen and learned to members of their communities. Over time, as they were passed from generation to generation, the shared revelations of these visionaries were transformed into religious dogmas.

DEFINING RELIGION

In the Ituri forests of Central Africa live the people known as the Mbuti Pygmies, a culture described in Colin Turnbull's classic book *The Forest People*.[1] They are still hunter-gatherers who also trade to some extent with the neighboring tribes for things they have come to need and enjoy, such as metal tools and agricultural crops. When the Mbuti are plagued by sickness or poor hunting, and when every practical remedy has failed, they hold a ceremony known as the *molimo*. For about a month, all the adult men gather nightly in their camp to sing and to rejoice in the forest. No specific invocations are made for better hunting or to end sickness. Their purpose is simply to express through song their trust in the forest as the benevolent provider of all good things. The molimo is held to awaken the forest to the Mbuti's presence and their plight and to restore harmony to their world. The Mbuti say that when harmony is restored, whatever happens next will be the will of the forest and that, therefore, it will be good.

Someone raised in the Judeo-Christian-Islamic tradition might not recognize the Pygmies' belief as being elements of a religion. No church or temple has been erected, and the molimo is not led by a priest or any other intermediary with the supernatural. In fact, the supernatural does not exist for the Mbuti as it does in our Western tradition. Not only is there no tangible or otherworldly power known as God, but the object of their intentions is exactly that which is most tangible and natural in the Mbuti's life: the forest environment.

An anthropologist, however, would perceive that the Mbuti beliefs and practices are a form of religion. Unlike the layperson in our Western world, the anthropologist does not define religion as the worship of God. Nor does the anthropologist try to sort out all the competing notions of gods that are part of humanity's various organized religious traditions.

If religion is not to be defined in terms of who or what is worshipped, how can it be defined? In general terms, all religions have two basic characteristics: (1) They include a dimension of the supernatural or sacred, and (2) they express an ideology.

Religion as Belief in the Supernatural

In 1912, the sociologist Emile Durkheim wrote a book, *The Elementary Forms of Religious Life*, in which he proclaimed that the essence of a religion is not a specific set of beliefs, practices, or attitudes but rather the expression of a community's moral values and collective beliefs, whatever these might be. This is what is known as a *cultural mythos*. Durkheim maintained that each society distinguishes between what he called the sacred and the profane—the sacred being that sphere of extraordinary phenomena associated with awesome supernatural forces, and the profane being the realm of the ordinary and the routine—the everyday world of physical reality.[2]

Religious beliefs express what a society considers to be sacred, and these beliefs, often expressed symbolically or mythically, become the focus of collective ceremonies that serve to unite believers into a single moral community. In this sense, the annual ceremonies of the Australian Aborigines that center around a Dreamtime hero are no less religious than the celebration of Easter or Yom Kippur or Ramadan.

Religion as Ideology

Some anthropologists have broadly defined religion as any system of beliefs, rituals, and symbols that make life meaningful and intelligible. Some maintain that religion is essentially an ideology, a system of very potent symbols that has a powerful emotional appeal and can provide a rationale for human existence. Religious ideology can thus be understood on two levels:

> ⚜ Religion provides a symbolic framework that allows us to understand our place in the universe. A number of anthropologists, including the esteemed Frenchman Claude Levi-Strauss, have argued that the symbolic expressions embodied in myths are arranged in a common pattern worldwide. This has been called the structuralist approach.

✳ Symbols come to represent the basic elements of human existence, and because of this, religious symbols themselves assume a crucial significance. The cross of Christianity, the Star of David, the star and crescent of Islam—all are powerful symbols over which wars have been fought and countless innocents have been sacrificed.

It is important to be aware that the phenomenon of religion was actually created by human thought and that "God" is a human concept that, from the shamanist perspective, is a misunderstanding of the original concept of Creator. (See chapter 3 and the discussion on theism below in this chapter.)

ANIMISM

In the nineteenth century, the English anthropologist Edward B. Tylor was one of the first to try to systematically explain religion. In 1871, he published a book titled *Primitive Culture*, in which he asserted that the foundation of all religion is found in the idea of the soul. He defined the soul as a personal supernatural essence that differs from the physical body. Tyler called this belief *animism* and suggested that primitive people applied the idea of a soul not only to humans but also to animals and plants and to inanimate objects like stones, clouds, lakes, and mountains.[3] A good example of animism is seen in the molimo ceremony of the Mbuti, who seek to connect with the soul or spirit of the forest, which, if it is so inclined, will respond.

The doctrine of animism suggests that everything, both animate and inanimate, possesses its own personal supernatural essence, or soul. The doctrines of hylozoism and panpsychism further reveal that everything, both animate and inanimate, is alive, conscious, and aware, to some degree.

Hylozoism is a viewpoint developed by the pre-Socratic philosophers that everything, both animate and inanimate, is alive in some sense. Panpsychism is the view that everything everywhere possesses consciousness, mind, or some kind of mind-like quality. The word *panpsychism* was coined by the Italian philosopher Francescao Patrizi in the sixteenth century.

ANIMATISM

One of Tylor's contemporaries, R. R. Marett, argued in 1909 in his book *The Threshold of Religion* that the concept of a soul was too sophisticated to have supplied the foundation for religion. He proposed that animism was preceded by another belief he called *animatism*, a belief in an impersonal supernatural force or power.[4]

Good examples of animatism are found everywhere. The peoples of Polynesia and Melanesia attribute unusual powers, as well as good luck and misfortune, to mana, an invisible force that can be transmitted by touch and may be gathered for good or evil, depending on the intentions of practitioners. The Algonkian Indians living around the Great Lakes of North America were in relationship with the manitou spirits, who came to warriors and medicine people in visions, endowing them with supernatural power. Roman Catholics believe in the healing powers of sacred relics of saints or locations, like Lourdes. The !Kung San bushmen of southern Africa work with *num*, a boiling energy that originates from the spirits and can endow those who possess it with healing energy. The belief in supernatural power or force is very widespread and is probably universal. In the West, we often call it "good luck."

THEISM

During the past five thousand years or more, human beings created stratified, state-level societies supported by intensified agriculture. The first organized religions devised by the first bureaucratized priesthoods and governments emerged in tandem. And as our perspective of ourselves became more centralized and stratified, so did our conceptions of the supernatural worlds, resulting in the first theist belief systems vested in supernatural gods and goddesses above and beyond nature.

The belief in the existence of spirits, or *theism*, is also probably universal, although the spirits are conceived of in very different ways. For example, among the Yoruba peoples of western Nigeria, there are over three hundred gods or spirits known as orisha, each of which has a strong personality and each of which was involved in the mythic past with an aspect of creation manifested into the natural world. They include Shango, the god of thunder; Obatala, the god of the skies; Yemoja, the goddess of the ocean; Oshun, the goddess of rivers; Ewa, the goddess of mists; Nana, the goddess of springs; and Ogun the god of iron.

This belief in many spirits or godlike beings is called *polytheism*, and in the Western world we are perhaps most familiar with the polytheist beliefs of the Egyptians, Greeks, Romans, and Celts. The Hindus, Norse, Saxons, Sumerians, Persians, Babylonians, Aztecs, Maya, Incas, and many other societies based in intensive agriculture also had well-developed polytheistic beliefs.

Examined carefully, the deities of these cultures are symbols in an ideological sense who are usually associated with some aspect of the natural world, beings with awareness and intelligence who can act in our world in a supernatural sense.

The belief in a single great father-god who created the universe and everything in it and all at once is known as *monotheism*.

The monotheist concept of God implies the existence of some high, divine, off-planet father-god entity outside of us that we must worship and to which we must defer. It is separate from and above us. The central deity in these traditions is variously known as Yahweh, Jehovah, Allah, or more generally God, and belief in this supreme being is the foundation for all three of the major monotheist traditions—Judaism, Christianity, and Islam—that took form in the deserts of the Middle East. In monotheist traditions, this deity is often designated as "the Creator," responsible for the manifestation of everything in the universe and also credited for watching over human affairs, sending occasional messengers to Earth, and working in mysterious ways.

This belief in a mono-god can really only be viewed as relative, as all expressions of monotheism deify (or reify) saints and prophets to some extent, and all have made room at various points in their histories for other supernatural beings: the djinn of the Middle East; the faerie folk of the Anglo-Saxons; and the saints, angels, and demons of Catholicism and Christianity in general.

Some anthropologists have suggested that these patterns of religious belief are related to the ways in which societies are organized. One such person is Guy E. Swanson, whose book *The Birth of the Gods: The Origin of Primitive Beliefs* suggests that animism tends to be found in less complex societies in which the nuclear family is the sovereign kin group, and social organization is in hunting-gathering bands or small rural agricultural hamlets.[5]

Polytheism by contrast is usually associated with societies in which there exist social classes with occupational specializations (jobs), and these classes are often organized into extended family systems with plural marriage. Monotheism is strongly associated with societies in which there is a high degree of social complexity, with politically important groups and social stratification resulting in considerable inequality among the levels. Once again, the nuclear family is the sovereign kin group.

Swanson suggests that the elites of monotheist societies invoke the power of the "high god" to preserve their privileges and prevent rebellion in the lower classes. He also suggests that religious belief systems seem to reflect the basic characteristics of the social order in which they appear, and as social organization becomes more stratified and centralized, so does our conception of the supernatural. This is interesting, as the reality spheres of the sacred and the profane seem to reflect each other. In other words, they are simply two halves of a whole. The gods didn't create us; we created them.

An Alternative Worldview

What makes the truths held by the mystics, visionaries, and shamans in the past any different from the beliefs held by our organized religions?

As I have indicated, there is indeed a supreme state of being that has been called the Originator. However, I have come to understand (see my "Journey to the Source" in *Visionseeker*) that this unitive level and the awareness it possesses is utterly impersonal and actually more of a dynamic dimension, one that continually emanates, as mentioned earlier. The mystery schools of the past revealed that it is not separate from us, but rather we are all a part of it in the sense that we are aspects of it rather than its subjects. As noted in chapter 3, none of the names given to this "being" by our religions, such as God, are its true name. If your religion requires that you think of it as your infinite creator, that's fine, but it doesn't require that you worship it. Rather, correct protocol suggests that we live in a state of gratitude for the All-That-Is and that we be in service to it.

It has also been my experience that the higher organizing intelligences, including those who are creators, do not require our worship. They want us to understand Creation, as well as our place within this universal dynamic. When we are honored by their connection with us, we experience their overarching compassion for us and their encouragement for us to become co-creators with them. This relationship is a large part of the reason for our re-enchantment and our sequential re-embodiments in the reincarnational cycle as we pursue our destiny in our long walkabout across time.

The mystics and shamans of the past asked us to take nothing on faith. Instead, they laid out a grand experiment in which each could verify these percepts by direct experience. The method is meditation, or shamanic journeywork, and the goal is to discover who and what we really are, as well as what we are doing here, what this world is all about, and where we fit into it. The mystery schools of the past expressed their teachings to those who were ready through direct revelation, through Gnostic perception, which was and is the path of the shaman. And this path is an aspect of the Master Game.

As I've pointed out, shamanism is not a religion, nor does it conflict with any of our established religions. It's a spiritual practice through which we can directly reconnect with the great mystery of life. And this reconnection often happens in response to our re-enchantment and our enhanced relationship with nature. For many visionaries, including me, direct experience with the natural world is intertwined with direct experience of the so-called supernatural.

Those who have read my books and essays about the worlds of the shaman and my own encounters with the supernatural, such as those described in chapter 1 (or in my Spiritwalker series, for that matter) may at times find it difficult to reconcile these accounts with what we have been taught about reality by our parents and friends, our teachers and religious authorities.

I must add that it is currently impossible for Western science to seriously consider the experiences I have shared in my books (including this one) as real, let alone to investigate or even validate them. Yet it was these encounters, achieved through direct revelation, that drew me, a scientist and an academic researcher, into the worlds of the shaman. Many well-educated and well-published people have traveled on this same visionary path in our time and have discovered for themselves the shaman's worldview.

And just what is the shaman's worldview?

Seeing with the Eyes of the Shaman

In opposition to the generally held belief that the physical level of objective reality is the only "real world," let me repeat that the shamans of traditional tribal peoples perceive reality to be a complex mosaic made up of two halves: an outer world of things seen and the inner worlds of things hidden. Shamans see and interact with both the ordinary reality of everyday life and the nonordinary realities, where the physical laws of nature and cause and effect may not apply. These nonordinary realities are synonymous with the Dreamtime of the Australian Aborigines and the other worlds, or the spirit worlds, of other traditional peoples.

Through my years spent living with traditional peoples, I would hear a statement repeated often and with great conviction: that the dream worlds are the eternal worlds, and everything that exists in our ordinary, everyday, and ever-changing life was sourced into existence from these spiritual dimensions. This statement implies that the dream worlds of spirit are the subtle and causal blueprint for our everyday world, so to speak, and that this world that we all take for granted is an ephemeral, ever-changing projection of those dimensions, a level of reality that is ever shifting in response to who and what we become and create in the here and now.

It is interesting that virtually all shamans in every culture perceive these dreamlike realms in the same way—as a multilayered assemblage organized into three great cosmic regions:

⚕ the Lower Worlds, which are the dreaming of nature;

⚕ the Middle Worlds, which are the dream aspect of our everyday world, as well as the dreaming of humans, and include the postmortem transitional worlds between life and the afterlife that the Tibetans call the Bardos; and

⚕ the Upper Worlds, or Sky Worlds, the dreaming of the gods and goddesses and the spiritual heroes and heroines of the past, including our ancestors, our higher selves, and the higher organizing intelligences generally known as the angelic forces.

In many cultures, these three transpersonal regions may be further subdivided based on who and what is found in each realm.

The shaman's worldview is remarkably consistent from culture to culture and is held in common by virtually all the peoples of planet Earth. It is of interest that science has been unable to invalidate this shamanic perspective of the world. Writer and investigative reporter Graham Hancock, in response to his own discoveries on the mystic road, observed that science has never been able to demonstrate that the way in which tribal shamans explain reality is wrong, nor has science been able to show that there is anything faulty or illogical about the shaman's worldview. In his seminal book, *Supernatural: Meetings with the Ancient Teachers of Mankind,* Hancock notes that the materialist paradigm, upon which all the progress and achievements of Western technology have been built, could likely face catastrophic implosion if the shaman's view of the universe were ever proved to be right.[6]

Researcher Rick Strassman, MD, concurs in his book *DMT: The Spirit Molecule: A Doctor's Revolutionary Research into the Biology of Near-Death and Mystical Experiences.* He points out that the spiritual dimensions cannot be accessed using our everyday state of consciousness. He and many others who have experienced them directly suggest that they are quite real, outside of us and freestanding, and that if we "simply change our brain's receiving abilities, we can apprehend and interact with them."[7]

In my experience as a Westerner, a scientist, a writer who was drawn into the shamans' worlds of mystery and magic through my own spontaneous visionary experiences, and as someone who has walked this path for more than thirty years, these inner worlds do indeed exist and they are all around us all the time. As Carl Jung suggested in the quote at the beginning of this book, the trick lies in learning how to perceive them.

It is also my guess that these so-called other worlds may be the parallel dimensions that advanced theoretical physics predicts. Like countless other Westerners and indigenous peoples who have had direct contact with these dimensions, I have experienced that these inner worlds "vibrate" at a different frequency from our own and are thus inaccessible to us except when we are in expanded states of consciousness or when we are dreaming. The ability to intentionally alter our consciousness and expand our perceptual awareness is and has always been in the realm of the shaman.

Furthermore, visionaries and shamans all over the world proclaim with their considerable authority that these hidden realities are inhabited by intelligent beings, some of whom have had an active interest in humanity for a very long time. These beings appear to get involved in human affairs most often as spirit helpers, spirit teachers, and Spirit Guides. They also appear to include our own higher self, often referred to as our oversoul, a term coined by the American poet and mystic Ralph Waldo Emerson.[8]

In *Supernatural,* Hancock notes that it is clear—from reading the Old Testament of the Bible or the Egyptian Book of the Dead, for example—that the visionary experiences of our religions' founders were not simply conjured up in someone's creative imagination. Nor were they arrived at through scholarly study or deliberately devised to assuage human needs.[9] Moreover, it is obvious that the founders' paranormal experiences were enabled by altered states of consciousness that have been part of human history and prehistory stretching back to the dawn of human awareness—experiences often facilitated by intense shamanic meditation in combination with prayer and drumming or rattling (sonic driving), by tantra (involving the deep erotic), and sometimes by entheogens (hallucinogens). Another powerful gateway into transcendence is through trauma, in which one may be precipitated into a classic near-death experience or out-of-the-body experience of the transitional Middle Worlds between life and the afterlife. Discussions of such paranormal experiences are well beyond the reach of this brief narrative, but they have been very well documented, and those who have had them and returned to tell about them now number in the thousands.

Hancock suggests that if we turn toward the organized religious traditions in the Western world, we can see that the original visionary experiences and revelations of their founders are now far back in the dimly remembered past. Since then, history has documented how the bureaucratized priesthoods of these traditions distorted, censored, and rewrote the original teachings and revelations of their founders to suit the political agendas of the times in which they lived. In our world today, our priests, rabbis, imams, and other religious leaders present themselves to us as the exclusive intermediaries between our communities and the supernatural. Yet with rare exceptions, most possess no visionary abilities themselves. In fact, most of them are no more likely than any other members of their communities to encounter the hidden worlds and the transpersonal forces that reside within them. Since my boyhood growing up nominally Episcopalian, I've watched these religious leaders rigidly adhere to scripture and teach what they themselves have been taught by other non-visionaries who relied on scripture. Hancock concurs, observing that those who direct and control our organized religions today will almost never convey any new transpersonal experiences of their own to enhance and refresh the original revelations of their religions' founders. There are exceptions, but they are rare.

Strong words? Perhaps, and yet the spiritually blind have for so long been allowed to mislead the spiritually blind about the very experiences and revelations that gave rise to our religious traditions in the first place. Hancock calls this one of the great tragedies of the modern world. He adds that our so-called paranormal abilities, which our indigenous ancestors long used with reverence and caution to explore and learn from the hidden worlds and their inhabitants, were intentionally diverted by our priestly bureaucrats into the various spiritual dead-ends of the ecclesia, where everything is dogma, endlessly repeated, and almost no one has firsthand experiences of the transpersonal realms anymore.[10]

Fortunately, evolution has offered us a truly great gift through which we may bypass all the fears and blocks inserted into us by our religious authorities at large and gain access to the Dreamtime once again for power and protection, for support and wisdom, for healing and problem solving. By walking the road of the inspired visionary, each of us may have access to the full spectrum of human consciousness and to the multiple realities available to us within the realm of things hidden. The real spiritual truths are there, waiting to be discovered, just on the other side of the mirror.

ENCOUNTERS WITH
THE NORTH WIND

As I have suggested, the ability to have the direct experience of the sacred realms appears to be one of our birthrights. These mystical perspectives are generally held by those gifted individuals who have directly experienced the hidden levels of reality through visionary revelations and who encounter the transpersonal forces that reside there, forces the traditional people call spirits. Here is an experience that clearly reveals what is possible when one is walking the shamanic path of direct revelation.

When I was a boy growing up in New York City, the fierce winter winds were a force to deal with, especially the north wind, which brought storms and blizzards and freezing temperatures. During this time (the 1940s), my mother read to me a wonderful book by a British author named George MacDonald, *At the Back of the North Wind*, a great children's fantasy written in the time of Queen Victoria.[1] This is a story in which the powerful and maternal north wind takes on a relationship with a little boy named Diamond, the son of a poor coachman. Diamond is transformed when "she" takes him on a visit into the world of things hidden, a beautiful country "at the back of the north wind." In response, the boy Diamond experiences what it is to be truly alive.

This is a shamanic adventure story in every sense, and, not surprisingly, my enchanted younger self took on an interesting and mysterious connection with the spiritual essence of the winds and the north wind in particular. Interestingly, I did not see the north wind in the manner of Arthur Hughes's original and powerful illustrations from the book. I did not see "her" as a flying superbeing with human features and tumultuous masses of wild hair. Rather, I perceived her as an immense, dark, amorphous form that towered over me, reaching up high into the sky . . . and curiously I remember that she had brilliant lights buried deep within her black smoky mass—the kind of lights produced by those sparklers we used to wave around as children on the Fourth of July.

I don't know why I saw the wind spirit in this way. I just did. This relationship withdrew for a time at childhood's end, and then it returned in response to my re-enchantment later in life, as revealed in the following account.

More than a decade ago, my family and I were living in a community near Sacramento in the Central Valley of Northern California. One summer, the temperatures soared for three weeks straight, never descending below 100 degrees Fahrenheit at night and reaching 117 to 120 degrees during the days. This was like being baked in an oven, and toward the end of this period I began to yearn for the north wind to return and cool things down. I waited, yet it wasn't her season and she didn't come.

Then one blistering day in September, I was in my study at home preparing my lecture for a late afternoon class at one of the colleges where I taught a course on the anthropology of religion. By chance I looked out the window and saw the leaves of the birch tree dancing. I immediately went outside and stood under the tree. The north wind had finally come.

I faced into the wind, spread out my arms and fingers, and closed my eyes. I opened my heart and welcomed her as I did as a child. For perhaps fifteen minutes I simply stood outside my house, accessing the shamanic state and letting her wind blow through and around me as whispered murmurings filled my ears. When I opened my eyes, I noticed several of the neighbors watching me with concern, so I gave them a cheery wave and pointed into the wind, giving them the thumbs up sign. This was a rather conservative community and they did not look reassured, so I retreated to my study. Shortly after, I drove to the college and offered my thoughts and insights on a topic that now eludes me to a packed lecture hall.

On this particular afternoon, something unusual happened. As the students left the hall at the end of class, I was approached by a young woman with dark hair and assumed she wanted to ask a question. She waited until the last students had left, then introduced herself and politely informed me that she had psychic abilities. I smiled and made encouraging gestures.

"I wonder if you know," she continued, "that in addition to your students, there are others who come to your class to hear what you have to say." "Others?" I asked. "Yes . . . others," she said. "I've always had psychic sight, even as a child. I discovered early on that my friends and family members couldn't handle it and so I rarely reveal who and what I am. But I've been absorbing your lectures for several weeks and thought you might find my perceptions interesting."

She went on. "Usually I see the 'others' in your class in human form. I sometimes see them as shadows or in black and white rather than color and believe them to be the discarnate spirits of deceased people who are still here in this world. They seem to be interested in what you talk about . . . and there are also others who are not human [she didn't elaborate]. Sometimes I also see the spirits of the people who once lived here, the Indians.

"But today there was one here I had never seen before." She watched me carefully and I could feel goose bumps forming on my arms. "It was like a huge dark black giant, a rather formless one with lights sparkling deep inside it. It reached all the way to the ceiling. As I studied the dark giant with some concern, it suddenly became aware that I could see it. It immediately became very deferential. I received a transmission from it, not so much in words as in impressions and impulses that just came to me. That tends to be how I 'see.' It revealed that it was not there to cause any trouble. Rather, it was curious about you." She paused as if to see the effect of her words. I watched her and nodded, remembering my encounter that afternoon.

"The dark spirit had a message for you. It indicated that it had known you for a long time and that there are more books that you need to write. It was almost as if it was saying 'keep writing.' And then there was something else." She paused again. "It told me to tell you that it is the bearer of healing energy and that it will come when you call it. It waited as if to see my reaction and then it just simply wasn't there anymore. It was gone."

I drew a long breath, smiled, and thanked her for her words, then she turned and departed and never spoke to me after class again.

A year or so later, I was leading a five-day workshop in shamanic healing practice at the Breitenbush Conference Center in the tall mountain forests of northern Oregon. It was July and breathlessly hot, and my thoughts turned often toward the north wind, but I knew this wasn't her season. One afternoon between sessions, I retreated to my rustic cabin, took off all my clothes, and sat for a while on my bed in light meditation. The workshop participants were going to do a full-on transpersonal healing ritual for one of the members that evening, and with these thoughts, I suddenly heard the hoot of an owl. The call penetrated my sense of meditative calm like a rifle shot.

Curious, I thought. Owls are nocturnal and I had never heard one call in these forests in the daytime before. I was almost settled when the owl hooted again. An understanding built within me, and I sensed that I was being called. As I pulled on my clothes, the hoot came again. I went outside and looked up into the trees, aware that it was highly unlikely that I would see the owl unless it wished to be seen.

It was then that I saw the leaves were dancing and I turned toward the north. I faced into the cooling breeze, extended my arms in welcome and felt gratitude welling up. The north wind had arrived for the healing ritual.

THE NEW MYSTERIES

I have long used the term *mystery* to describe strange yet dramatic episodes in my life that cannot be adequately described or intellectually understood. I came to associate these encounters with a phenomenon that I have referred to earlier as "the Mystery." For me, these encounters were life changing, and in my Spiritwalker series, as well as in this book, I've shared some of them. Looking back, I sense today that the Mystery, an elusive presence that is always there, may both attract and intrigue us, and possibly draw us forward toward that which we are destined to become. Perhaps this is its function.

One of the most well-known mystery schools of the pre-Christian world was in the Greek village of Eleusis, near Athens, which was dedicated to the earth goddess Demeter and her daughter, Persephone, who became the part-time wife of Hades, the lord of the Lower Worlds. There exists a plethora of writings about the spiritual trainings, rites, and initiations performed at Eleusis, and John Lamb Lash, in *Not in His Image*, has described much of what went on there in the classical period. In his words, "Initiates of the mysteries realized that the goddess requires of those to whom she reveals herself the humility to admit that they cannot fully know what it means to be human without the inspired guidance of non-human beings."[1]

This is an important insight and probably could be applied to most of the mystery schools that existed in the past. The shamans' visionary methodology lay right at the heart of all their spiritual practices. Many of these great schools of philosophic thought (Egypt, for example) lasted for thousands of years, and yet all were systemically destroyed in very short order with the emergence of the monotheist religious complex of Christianity seventeen hundred years ago.

As I have said in the preceding chapters, I believe that the essence of the ancient mysteries may be re-emerging in our own time in a new form in response to our need for them, in the process morphing to reflect who we are today. At the center of this new spiritual complex lies the realization that each one of us can make the direct, transpersonal connection with the hidden realms of spirit. Once we do, we can become our own priest or priestess, our own guru or teacher, our own prophet, receiving revelations directly from the hidden inner worlds without the intrusion of any intermediary religious organization, priesthood, or cult, in confirmation of Lash's statement above.

As mentioned earlier, I am not a theologian or a therapist, nor am I a priest. Rather, I am a scientist whose research drew me more than forty years ago into the arid, eroded landscapes of southwestern Ethiopia, where I began to have spontaneous and unsought visionary experiences that would expand my awareness into regions of consciousness largely unexplored by either the academic world or our mainstream religious traditions. And how was I to talk about these experiences with my academic colleagues—or with anyone else, for that matter?

I was aware that my fellow scientists were not ready to consider, let alone discuss, what I had to share, and so I eventually decided to write about my explorations into the "forbidden zones" that reside beyond the horizons of both organized religion and science. The books in my Spiritwalker series are quite different from my scientific publications, to say the least. And now, at more than seventy-five years of age, I feel an inner stirring, a response perhaps from my soul source that resides within my heart as I turn my attention toward the New Mysteries, toward the possibility of a new spiritual operating system available to us all.

The visionary path of the shamanist is inclusive. It is intensely democratic and potentially available to everyone rather than exclusive for some. It is intuitive and experiential and interactive in direct contrast to the unquestionable doctrine trumpeted by the dogmatized priests of our increasingly outdated monotheist religions, which are exclusionist. I might observe once again (and dispassionately) that the moment has truly come for us to create a new cultural mythos—a new story that will redefine who we are, who we can be, and who and what we wish to become. This new mythos is essential in creating a new world that we wish to pass on to our grandchildren and to their grandchildren.

If I were to draw upon the observations of the Hawaiian elder Hale Makua, this new world order will be determined by where we, as individuals and as a culture, choose to sink our anchor. From his perspective, most of us have been firmly anchored in the "negative polarity" over the past several decades. But what does that mean? In his words, recorded in *The Bowl of Light*, "When love moves out, fear moves in."[2] And in response, we have experienced the negative polarity at its worst: economic bondage and enslavement, political deception and coercion, mendacity from our business leadership and from the media, massive and collective greed from the wealthy, misguided religious zeal and terrorist attacks, and tyranny from our political and military leaders who have been controlling the populace through manipulation and fear. How would this all change if we as individuals and as a culture were to lift anchor and re-sink it into the positive polarity? How would this affect the quality of our lives as well as the quality of our leadership at all levels?

Spirituality in our time is being redefined as something quite distinct from what has historically been offered from our organized religions. It is through direct mystical experience that we may establish an ongoing and intimate contact with our spirit guardians and with our immortal spiritual aspect: our oversoul, or higher self.

The Oversoul and the Spirit Guide

I often wonder whether our political problems have political solutions, whether our economic problems have economic solutions, if our social problems have social solutions, and if our religious divisions have religious solutions, and so forth. If so, it is hard to see them, but I do see the possibility for spiritual problems having spiritual solutions, and among these solutions rests the transformationals' awareness of and relationship with the transpersonal forces (spirits) who are supporting us and want the best for us.

It is generally understood and accepted in the modern mystical movement that each of us has a higher self. Some, like the visionary Thomas Moore, refer to it as our spirit, as the immortal aspect of ourselves who lives forever in the dreaming. Some refer to it as our soul. Ralph Waldo Emerson referred to it as the oversoul. The Hawaiian elder Hale Makua called it 'Aumakua (with a capital A), our utterly trustworthy ancestral spirit. Many indigenous people and modern mystics alike understand it to be our spiritual soul from whom we are sourced into each life. As such, it is one of our three souls, a triune complex we shall consider shortly. At this point, let us observe also that the oversoul is not our Spirit Guide.

Understood correctly, our Spirit Guide is a member of that grand company of spiritual beings that many visionaries call "the higher organizing intelligences." I and many others think of them in this way because of our collective experience that the outstanding characteristic of the spirit worlds is a continuous feeling of a powerful mental force that is directing everything and creating a state of harmony. The Guides (who can be considered as members of the angelic forces) seem to be the ones responsible for generating this sense of balance and tranquility.

From the shamanist perspective, each one of us has a Spirit Guide (with a big G) who is a figure of grace, a godlike being who resides in the Upper Worlds and who is involved in our immortal oversoul's continuing evolution and growth. The Guide is part of the fulfillment of our personal and collective destiny as we continue to travel across time, growing, increasing, and becoming more in response to each life. The Guide is our oversoul's caretaker and teacher to whom we were assigned when we came into being as a soul.

In my experience, my Spirit Guide rarely gets involved in the mundane details of my everyday life although it sometimes does step in. Through meditation, through spontaneous insight and through dreaming, some of us discover the existence of our Guide as well as its interest in us, and we often learn that we have more than one Guide. For example, our senior Guide may have a younger junior Guide in training. We may also discover through direct experience and through comparing notes with others that the Guides' teaching styles may vary considerably, yet they appear to support and interface beautifully with our permanent oversoul matrix. Some of us also have established relationships with the oversoul fields of ascended masters, such as Yogananda or Merlin. Hale Makua had a relationship with Metatron, the chief of the angelic forces.

It has also been my experience that most spiritual seekers who use the terms *guide* or *guides* are actually referring to their helping spirits, those earthbound beings who provide us with power, protection, support, and information. These spirit helpers function more as guardians and are often perceived as power animals, nature spirits, elementals, or plant teachers. However, they can also appear to us in human form, sometimes as an ancestor, sometimes as someone else. These spirit helpers are lower in the spiritual hierarchy and are not Guides, per se, although shamanists discover that they can and will provide teachings to us, especially in the early stages of our relationship with them.

The Spirit Guides, correctly understood, are high-level spiritual beings who have great and enduring compassion for their oversoul charges. In this perspective, our Spirit Guide is a master teacher with whom our personal and immortal higher self/ oversoul is in relationship as its "student." The Guide's teachings enhance the life lessons that we as embodied manifestations of our oversoul are here to learn. And the goal? When we have learned those lessons, there is no repeat, and both our mortal incarnational self and our immortal oversoul self are enhanced in response to what we have done and become in this life. Then we move on to more lessons.

It has been my experience that our Guides are not judgmental; this is an important point because this is not, nor has it ever been, a punitive system. There are no lords of karma who judge and condemn us. That is a myth designed to control people. However, we learn through visionary experience that each of us does have a Council of Wise Elder Spirits. These are higher beings who reside in the Upper Worlds, a kind of "cosmic committee" that debriefs us when we return from a life just lived and briefs us again before we return to the next. They are the ones who hold our "cosmic contract," the agreement that extends out to each of us the path of our destiny, including, of course, our life lessons upon which we are currently working. They are exalted Guides who have great respect for who we are, as well as the soul age at which we currently exist, and we will be given many second chances if at first we do not succeed in learning our lessons. We meet with them between lives several times to discuss our progress and to explore how we might do better. They also help us to decide on the shape of our next life and how this life will interface with the lessons on which we are currently working. They help build morale by foreseeing great things for us.

The excellent books of Michael Newton, PhD, and those of his colleague Linda Backman, PhD, reveal much about the interlife state and how some Guides constantly help their students' embodiments on earth, while others take the hands-off approach, insisting that we work on our life lessons with little or no encouragement. Both Newton and Backman point out that graduate students—those of us who are older in our soul age—seem to get less help than freshmen, those who are younger souls.[3]

And here is something curious. I have been shown that when Spirit Guides choose to reveal themselves to us, they may often appear as figures in our faith—a Christian seeing Jesus, a Jew meeting with Moses, or a Muslim encountering the prophet Mohammed or the archangel Gabriel. This well-documented phenomenon may explain why many in the Christian community who have had a near-death experience have had a visionary connection with a being whom they interpret as Jesus. The Guides do not have bodies; they are energetic in nature. Yet they know that if they appear to us as spiritual beings with whom we are already familiar, we may be more inclined to come into relationship with them. Thus, those who encounter Jesus or Moses or Mohammed may actually be in the presence of their Guide who has taken this form to make an impression. Sometimes, however, the Spirit Guides appear to us as they really are—as the light beyond the form, and the formless beyond the light, infused with a vast intelligence tempered by an omnipresent compassion for us. We discover through direct experience that they are in relationship with us to help us, but we also learn that correct protocol requires that we ask them for that help.

More than two hundred years ago, the well-known Seneca Indian medicine man Handsome Lake had a spiritual encounter with what he described as a blue being surrounded by a halo of light who told him that the spirits had decided to help the Indians survive the genocide being inflicted upon them by the colonials. This blue being was his Spirit Guide who gave him a new code of laws for his people that became known as the Code of Handsome Lake. In response, the Seneca, as well as other nations in the Iroquois Confederacy, survived and flourished.[4]

One of the key functions performed by these wise beings has traditionally been to provide humans with teachings and initiations of various kinds, some of which can be quite challenging. Ethnographic literature reveals that they are involved with the transference of knowledge to those spiritual seekers who are deemed ready to receive it. They may also bring us into connection with others in the spiritual hierarchy, so we may discover that we have more than one teacher. This is the shaman's path and practice in every sense.

This is a summary of what is actually a complex topic and reveals that there are two primary gateways into the spiritual worlds: the practice of Nature Mysticism—which connects us with the elementals, the spirits of nature and other earthbound forces—and the practice of Deity Mysticism, through which each one of us is involved with two primary and immanent levels of "deity," our oversoul and our Guide, and all the time.

The Spirit Guide is a higher level of deity, the one who draws us up and into the higher levels of the spiritual hierarchy where we may connect with other higher beings when we are deemed ready. We are all going in this direction, no matter who we are and what we are engaged with during our current life or what our religious belief systems may be. This passage of ascent, of growth upward into who and what we are destined to become as we travel across eternity as souls, is always and forever a readiness issue.

The second but foremost level of deity is our own immortal higher self, our oversoul, our god-self who serves us as the source of our intuition and inspiration and from whom we receive dreams and visions and ideas. Sometimes we experience connection with it as that still small voice within that may function as a companion, an adviser, and a spiritual companion who provides us with information in response to our need to know. It is often the one with whom we converse when we are "talking to ourselves." This reveals that our oversoul serves us during life as our primary spirit teacher. When you establish an ongoing and intimate relationship with your oversoul and with your Spirit Guide, they become your two best friends, far above and beyond any other relationships in your current life.

And by the way, both your personal oversoul and your Spirit Guide have names. These names are something for you to discover. In response to having visionary connections with them, you will learn that they cherish and love you unconditionally and that there is nothing to fear. And they will provide you with teaching and information and guidance about your personal destiny as a soul, about the life lessons upon which you are currently working, about the world's problems and your personal responsibilities, and so forth. But only if you ask.

THE NEW PERSPECTIVE OF GOD

In contrast to the archaic and mythic monotheist view of a father-god who lives off-planet and who has good days and bad days, the direct experience of the modern visionary reveals that our oversoul is, in fact, our personal "God in Heaven," the one who actually listens to our prayers, works in mysterious ways, and sends us to Earth as occasional messengers who sometimes get treated badly.

Several years ago, Wayne Dyer said to Oprah Winfrey on her daytime talk show SuperSoul Sunday, "The soul is the deathless part of us—the part that looks out from behind our eyes and has no form." And when Oprah asked him for his definition of God, Wayne replied, "God is the highest place within each and every one of us. It's our divine self."[5] Dyer realized that the true self within each one of us is God. It is wise and powerful. It is also good. He also knew something that Carolyn Boyes-Watson and Kay Pranis have revealed in their book *Heart of Hope: A Guide for Using Peacemaking Circles to Develop Emotional Literacy, Promote Healing & Build Healthy Relationships*—that to live from this core self, which represents the best in us, requires practice.[6]

Dyer's insights reveal an eternal truth—that our oversoul is our own immortal wise spirit being, our divine self, the god who loves us unconditionally and who is always in connection with us. The noble Emerson understood that our oversoul is, and forever will be, our guardian angel, our personal god who increases, grows, and becomes more in response to what we, its embodiments, do and become here on the physical plane of action through countless lives on our long journey across time.

The modern shamanist discovers through direct revelation that this extraordinary dynamic is a co-creative relationship between Heaven (our oversoul spirit self) and Earth (our embodied physical self). And it has been the experience of countless workshop participants that our personal oversoul exists as a composite etheric field made up of all of our former selves who lived former lives in former embodiments. Each of these "selves" continues to exist within our oversoul matrix, preserving a record, an energetic template of everything that we did and became during those lives as we worked on our life lessons here on the physical plane of planet Earth across eons of time.

When fully understood and accepted, this eternal truth reveals that the oversoul is our personal ancestral god-being to which we all may have access, whether through our dreaming, meditation, past-life regression therapies, hypnosis, or goal-oriented shamanic journeywork while very much awake. This revelation provides us with a new perception of God.

On July 14, 1930, the Indian mystic and poet Rabindranath Tagore visited Albert Einstein in Germany. During their talk, Tagore commented to Einstein, "My religion is in the reconciliation of the superpersonal self, the universal spirit, in my own individual being."[7] This superpersonal self is the oversoul and it is not human, by the way. It is simply a soul. It is the physical body we inhabit that is human.

To give you a visual image from my own experience, you might imagine your oversoul to be organized much like a child's Slinky toy laid out on its side on a flat surface with the ends of the coiled column joined. As such, the higher self takes the form of a tightly woven basket of circular energy strands, which appears to the mystic eye like a brilliant doughnut, or torus, made of light, one that may be laterally compressed, making it taller and forming a sphere, a (huge) orb-like ball of light.

The hole in the doughnut runs from top to bottom of the sphere and sometimes (but not always) creates a dense vertical shaft of light within the comparatively dimmer radiance of the basket itself. Each strand of the Slinky, each circular line or coil of light around the periphery and through the hole of the doughnut, represents an energetic disc somewhat like a DVD that records everything from the lifetime of a former self. Inside the torus is an energetic core that contains the distinct shape of our immortal character that we have developed through our embodiments across time, one that continually grows and changes as we become more (or less) during each life. The visionary artist Alex Grey has created a striking image of it in his book *Sacred Mirrors: The Visionary Art of Alex Grey*. He calls it the Universal Life Lattice.[8]

Through visionary perception, our oversoul is revealed to be the creative god-source from which we come into each life, and the central, vertical shaft of light within its field is often seen in deep meditation by mystics as a prominent landmark within the sphere. This may suggest why the Hawaiians and the Andean peoples, for example, have often used the vertical symbol of the standing stone for the creative god-principle—the mythic Kane in Hawai'i and the lord of light, Wirakocha, in South America. And since standing stones are found all over the world, perhaps this reveals what the symbol actually meant to those who placed these monoliths upright in antiquity.

A vertical shaft of light within a globe of dimmer radiance—this is what I have been shown in my own meditative journeywork to be the energetic morphology of my immortal spirit self-aspect—a field report, if you will, and I share this percept with you in order to give you a greater sense of it, extending as always a gentle invitation for you to engage in your own visionary fieldwork. This being is the immortal god who loves you. Unconditionally.

And the dreaming? *Dreaming* is a verb, implying a continuous flow of an ongoing process. This is a good way to describe the spirit world, which, in fact, dreaming is. In *The Bowl of Light*, I write that our heart appears to be the portal that gives us access to our oversoul field, which resides within the dreaming. So the question comes up for our consideration: Who is dreaming? As Hawaiian elder Hale Makua so wisely pointed out to me, it is none other than our oversoul who serves us our personal creator at the beginning of life and the repository to which our soul complex returns at the end of each reincarnational cycle. It is our oversoul who lives forever in the Dreamtime and who dreams, and who is dreaming right now, even as I write these words where I am, and you read them wherever you are. And there is more.

THE THREE SOULS

In most of my books I have addressed the reincarnation cycle and the indigenous perception that each one of us possesses not one but three distinct souls. Ultimately, all three souls originate from the same source, but they exist in very different states of quality. The spiritual traditions of the Hawaiians, the Inuit, the Lakota, the Cherokee, the Vodou peoples, and even the Shuar of the Amazon confirm this. How widely these percepts were once held among the indigenous peoples cannot be ascertained today, as so much has been lost due to the invasive and destructive influence of Christian missionary activity.

As I shared in *The Bowl of Light*, the kahuna tradition of Polynesia holds that prior to life, our oversoul divides itself, expressing a seed of its light (the bowl of light) that enters its new embodiment for a new life when we emerge from our mother's body and draw our first breath that the Hawaiians call the *Hā*—the divine breath of life.

The breath is the vehicle of transfer for this immortal soul seed and this principle is in complete alignment with the beliefs of all three of our monotheistic religions that proclaim "God breathes life into form." In fact, the word for *breath* and the word for *spirit* is the same in Latin (*spiritus*) as well as in Hebrew and Arabic (*ruach*). Yet when we walk on the mystic road, we discover that the one who breathes life into us is not some fatherly mono-god. It is actually our personal oversoul, our god-self in the Upper Worlds of spirit.

When our spirit soul seed arrives within us from that source with that first breath, it encounters a distinct and separate soul already in residence. This is our physical body soul that was sourced to us by our mother through her egg and by our father through his sperm. In the same manner that these gametes, these sex cells, carry a genetic template that comes together to form the new and unique personal pattern of our DNA (half from the mother and half from the father), they also carry a psychic energetic template. This template is the initial source of our energy body with which the divine spark from the spirit soul now merges to create a unity. In other words, our energy body is derived from three sources, or ancestral lineages: our mother's lineage, our father's lineage (containing all maternal and paternal ancestral imprints), and our personal spiritual oversoul (containing all our spiritual ancestral imprints from past lives).

The physical soul functions as the source of our emotions and feelings, which is why some call it the emotional body. It is the human animal soul template within which our memories are recorded. It expresses our collective personality. It also carries the evolutionary software to operate, maintain, restore, and heal the physical body, and it is the aspect of ourselves that perceives both that which is seen in the objective outer world and that which is thought, felt, or dreamed in the subjective inner worlds.

The body soul is the interface between our "personal self" and "the other," revealing that the visionary portal into the spiritual worlds lies within it. The body soul is thus the sender and receiver of all psychic, shamanic, and mystic experiences, including those connections with our higher self. It takes everything literally, and like a good servant or personal computer, the body soul does what it is told.

And who tells it what to do?

This is our third soul who comes into existence in response to life as we lead it. We literally create a new one in each life. This is our mental soul, or egoic intellectual self, who will grow into wisdom as we mature, the one who will guide us successfully or unsuccessfully through life according to the beliefs and convictions that it holds to be true. As our inner director, the mental soul thinks, analyzes, assigns meaning to, practices discernment, makes decisions, and serves as the source of our intentionality and our creative imagination. It is through this last function that it can create thought-forms of things or achievements that it wishes to acquire. And through its will, it directs the activities of the body soul to enable the manifestation of these goals. The mental egoic soul is our inner CEO.

There is a strongly held and popular belief among New Agers that we have to drop or get rid of our ego. This, in my opinion, is an error of truly epic proportions, and no spiritual teacher who has experienced authentic initiation would ever make such a proclamation. Seen in the truth of its functions as listed in the previous paragraph, should we really get rid of our egos? The answer is obvious. Absolutely not!

Our egoic mental soul is our creative aspect, our inner chief, and it is the key to having a successful life as well as making the necessary decisions that enable us to achieve the life lessons we are here to experience and learn. When fully aware, our mental soul may also respond to messages sent from our oversoul. While being creative, it can also create a "default ego," the aspect of ourselves that can lie and create false selves and personalities with their own agendas. This is always a challenge, and it may be why some feel the need to demonize the ego.

Our immortal higher self, on the other hand, is the wise spiritual being (the first level of deity) who serves us as the source of our intuition and inspiration, the one who sends us dreams and visions as well as ideas and impulses in response to our need to know. Thomas Moore, in his seminal book *A Religion of One's Own: A Guide to Creating a Personal Spirituality in a Secular World*, reveals that the word *intuition* comes from a Latin word that means "to keep watch over." He observes, "Intuitions come and go quickly. You have to watch for them. They are like subtle messages coming at you, but so delicate and thin that you might easily let them go by. You have to learn to sort them out and eventually trust them."[9]

The word *trust* reaffirms that our oversoul is the one who is in service to us as our spirit teacher, and like its own teacher, the Spirit Guide, it may assume forms meaningful to us in our dreams and visions. This also suggests that our own best teacher, as the Hawaiian mystic Hale Makua always affirmed, is ourselves. The oversoul connects with our mental soul through the interface of the body soul. Our egoic intellect may then consider those impulses coming in because as the decision maker it serves us as our "chooser." It can choose to respond to spiritual insight or not. This is always and forever a readiness issue involving our capacity for free will.

It is generally known that the classical Greek philosopher and mathematician Pythagoras was the first in the Western tradition to offer his thoughts about these three *principias*—the three principle levels of body, mind, and spirit. His percepts then affected the thoughts of countless philosophers and visionaries across the centuries and take form in our own time as Sigmund Freud's id, ego, and superego, and Carl Jung's subconscious, conscious, and super-conscious minds. The Greeks subsumed two of these souls into one: the psyche, which they considered from their perspective to be the organ of both thought and emotion. From the indigenous perspective, however, these two quite separate functions are clearly products of two quite separate souls.

At life's end, the physical body dies. But what happens to your energy body? Nothing! The laws of thermodynamics reveal that energy cannot be created or destroyed, but it can shift to a new state. Energy is immortal, and the research of Michael Newton and Linda Backman, as well as the experiential knowledge of countless shamans, reveal that your personal triune soul complex—spiritual, mental, and physical—survives the death of the body and travels into the transitional dimensional level of the Middle World of dream carried by your energy body. This is what "in transition" means. During its stay in the Middle World, the soul complex may maintain its integration as a personal pattern, and many things may transpire. At the culmination of this period, it ascends in the company of your Spirit Guide and remerges with its source, your oversoul field, your great sphere of light that resides forever in the dreaming of the Upper Worlds of spirit. When this occurs, the oversoul enfolds into itself everything that you have ever thought, felt, done, and endured in the life just led, in response to which it grows, increases, and becomes more.

I have discussed the Originator, the ultimate Source of all being, including ourselves (see chapter 3). The Taoists understand that the Originator, which they call the Tao, continuously emanates parts of itself outward and downward through the various dimensional densities, and in response, a great game comes into being, one in which we are all players. This is the Master Game. It begins with our having forgotten who we really are, yet there exists an impulse within us, a yearning for something ineffable. We thus discover that our task, part of our mission as players of the game, is to remember and to know ourselves once again as aspects of the Originator who are growing and becoming more on our long journey home across space and time, bearing the gifts of everything that we have become.

From the visionary perspective, pain and suffering are just aspects of the game. They feel extremely real while we are playing, and indeed they have to in order to make us understand that the game is real. Our purpose in the game is to grow, develop, and transform ourselves into more positive and loving beings. We all have certain goals that we always plan to achieve before incarnating here on earth, which is why we pass through the veil of forgetfulness in returning to life. If we already knew what our goals were, the game would be too easy and there would be no growth.

Many spiritual teachers encourage us to look at the things in our life that we most love, those that make us happy. It is good for us to experience these as often as possible, as they will reveal some of the things that are included on our soul contract for this life. It is also important to look at the negative experiences that often seem to recur during our lifetime. It is likely that these are also life lessons on which we chose to come here to work.

All manner of circumstances in life will test us. Once we have successfully identified these issues and used them as the tools of transformation to improve the quality of our character, we notice that negative things seem to disappear from our life. We will still be presented with them at varying intervals to check and see that we have not forgotten that which we have learned, but they will be fewer and farther in between.

At the end of physical life, the visionaries among us know that no one really dies. My spirit teacher once said to me that at death, the matter of human form is shed, much like the chrysalis of a caterpillar, and then the butterfly, the spirit being that we really are, re-emerges to resume residence in the worlds of things hidden, where it eventually ascends and remerges with our spiritual oversoul in the "higher densities" (Hale Makua's term) of the afterlife state.

These insights reveal that we are truly immortals traveling across time. This includes all of us, and one thing is for sure: nobody fails. At the end of all our life cycles, both physical and nonphysical, all of us will eventually find our way Home to become one with the Originator once again. We will all get there and when we do, we will know what it knows and feel what it feels. We will become gods, and in this sense the Originator could be considered as a God being, I suppose. Yet there is so much political diatribe around the *God* word, and about who and what God is, says, or isn't, that a better term might simply be *Source*, which it is—the Source of all the dimensional levels of the spirit worlds and the Dreamtime, causal and subtle, the physical and nonphysical worlds, and everything that is found within them. When one considers the immensity of the universes infused everywhere with the life force, this is quite something, don't you think?

Nature Mysticism and Deity Mysticism

In our time and in response to such insights, spirituality is changing and shifting away from how our mainstream monotheist traditions have previously defined it. Having taught a university and college-level course in the anthropology of religion for many years, I've examined many of the world's mystical traditions and have come to the conclusion that there are many gateways into the spiritual worlds, though there appears to be two primary windows—Nature Mysticism and Deity Mysticism.

Many, if not most, of the world's indigenous people and Western people alike use the gateway of Nature Mysticism. For example, among the pre-Christian tribal peoples of Britain and Europe, there lived a shamanist priesthood who the Gauls called the Druides. In the classical period they came to be known as the Druids, and history reveals that they were highly organized into a hierarchy that included both men and women.

The Druids believed passionately in reincarnation and our personal immortality as a soul, percepts that lay right at the heart of their practices and teachings. Like most of the world's traditional tribal peoples, they were also keen observers of nature, and their knowledge of natural and universal processes was unequaled in the Roman and classical Greek worlds. They understood that the universe itself is indestructible. They also knew from direct revelation that what monotheists call "God" is not some supernatural god-father but rather a process that is densely concentrated in all living beings and thus within all of nature. In this sense, they knew that *God* is not a noun; it is a verb, a pantheistic revelation in which God is literally within everything everywhere as the life force, affirming that the shamanic tradition is the heritage of all those descended from the Anglo-Saxon-Gaulish-Celtic-Germanic-Norse peoples of Britain and Europe.

The Druids also served their tribal societies as judiciaries, as mediators who had the power to stop conflicts between competing tribes, families, or powerful individuals, and who dispensed justice from their vast knowledge of tribal and natural law, affirming the important role shamans traditionally held in tribal societies. Unlike our current judiciary in the United States today, the Druids were said to be immune to political or economic influence of any kind or at any level.

The Druids were the counselors of kings, respected visionaries and prophets, and supervisors of important religious rituals. Noble children were instructed by them, and oaths sworn before them. They were the wisdom keepers of their peoples, and for them the gateway into the transpersonal realms lay in the practice of Nature Mysticism, with the many aspects of nature itself, including their own bodies, serving as the doorways into the other worlds. Their teachings included knowledge of the motion of the stars, the size of the earth and the whole universe, the ordering of nature as well as the cosmic order, the power and nature of the gods, and why the universe behaves the way it does. In other words, they were highly educated people.[10]

It was through Nature Mysticism that I was able to find a spirit helper for my friend Mark, bringing him into relationship with a power animal who will continue to provide him with power, protection, and support . . . as well as information, for it has been my experience that the great serpent is the personification of superior wisdom and learning, quite in opposition to the demonism of the serpent archetype propounded by and through fundamentalist Christianity.

Another window into the spiritual worlds is the practice of Deity Mysticism. Deity Mysticism is different from Nature Mysticism in that it deals with a higher dimensional level from the dreaming of nature and the Middle Worlds of dream. An example of Deity Mysticism can found in the spiritual practices of the Tibetan Buddhist tradition that, by the way, are quite different from those of the older Hinayana or later Mahayana Buddhist traditions of India, the Theravada traditions of

Southeast Asia, as well as the traditions of Ch'an Buddhism in China and Zen Buddhism in Japan.

The Tibetan tradition combines Indian Buddhist thought and practices introduced from the south with the ancient Bon Po shamanistic practices that already existed in Central Asia to the north. Buddhism plus shamanism: this provides an interesting combination of mystical contemplation and visionary experience. The merger of the two, often referred to as the Vajrayana tradition, is thus unique.

The shamanist influence can be clearly seen in some of the spiritual practices in which the Tibetans engage and especially with Deity yoga, or what could be called Deity Mysticism. In these practices, the yogi (the practitioner) in deep meditation (contemplation) creates a mental image or thought-form (visioning) of a powerful deity such as Avalokiteshvara, the Himalayan bodhisattva of compassion, also known as Kwannon in Japan and Kwan Yin in China. Through ongoing and committed meditative practice, the yogi conjures up this deity day after day, projecting it outward, whereupon he or she then visualizes stepping forward and intentionally merging with the deity.

In Deity yoga, the practitioner becomes one with the deity, speaking, thinking, emoting, acting, and behaving as if they are embodying that powerful archetypal force. In the process, they find themselves accessing profound wisdom, expressing boundless compassion, and behaving with endless virtue in every thought and feeling, action and reaction, as they pass through their daily life. This practice is similar to shamanism in which the shaman, in trance, may merge with a power animal or spirit teacher, embodying that transpersonal force and in the process acquiring that being's abilities and knowledge.

It is understood by both the shaman and the yogi that these immortal transpersonal forces (deities), who have always been in relationship with us, are willing to constellate within and through us as vehicles in response to our invitation for them to do so, enabling them to manifest effects into our world that can be truly startling as well as life changing. The Tibetans say that through the practice of Deity yoga, an individual can become a Buddha, an awakened one, in a single lifetime instead of the three countless eons that this process would ordinarily take.[11]

I have been told that His Holiness the Dalai Lama practices Deity yoga daily, merging with the Himalayan deity of compassion, Avalokiteshvara. This means that should you ever have the honor to meet with His Holiness face to face, you will be in the presence of Avalokiteshvara. It will be this godlike being who speaks to you on his breath and who looks into your soul through his eyes.

As modern visionaries, we can adapt this practice, intentionally connecting with and becoming one with our oversoul, and we can do this at any time, any place. In other words, each of us has the ability to become one with and behave like a godlike being. This is what some spiritual seekers call "ascension," a process that becomes inevitable for us as we grow up and into the spiritual hierarchy of the higher worlds.

Allow me to share with you an account of an encounter with one such higher being from my own life, one that was both spontaneous and quite unexpected, an example of Deity Mysticism that did not happen in a church or temple or zendo or any other holy place. It happened in an airport.

Early one morning many years ago, I was sitting at a boarding gate watching the constant stream of my fellow travelers parading by, all like me on their way to somewhere. Some looked worried, preoccupied, or depressed while others appeared alert, determined, or excited. Many seemed tired, as though they were carrying burdens.

I glanced at the woman sitting next to me in the long row of seats near my gate. She was dressed in a black pantsuit and red blouse, black low-heeled shoes, and wearing subdued yet expensive gold jewelry, including a Patek-Phillipe watch. Her coifed and frosted hair was cut short, controlled and chic, and she was completely oblivious to my presence. She was scanning that day's copy of *The Wall Street Journal* with professional intensity through miniature folding reading glasses. Her carry-ons consisted of a laptop, an attaché case, and a small purse, suggesting that she was an attorney or businesswoman, perhaps. She was dressed for success and around her neck was a small Christian cross on a thin gold chain.

By comparison, I was wearing a black turtle-neck pullover, wrinkled khaki slacks, a dark olive green corduroy coat, and comfortable slip-on shoes. My hair under my soft tan safari-type hat was thinning on top but long and curly on the sides and in the back, and I was sporting a drooping moustache connected to a graying goatee. I was wearing Johnny Depp–type glasses, and my jewelry consisted of my three gold wedding rings and my father's gold signet ring. Around one wrist I wore the brass tribal bracelet given to me by the indigenous tribal man in the early 1970s complemented by a cheap Swiss Army watch around the other. Around my neck hung an old Maasai bead of warthog ivory on a black leather thong that came to me down in the Rift Valley on a blazing afternoon in Kenya. My carry-on was a weathered shoulder bag stuffed with books and papers, chocolate bars, and a cell phone I rarely used, with a collapsible umbrella stuck in a sleeve on one end and a water bottle in the sleeve on the other. I also had my portable office, a roller bag with a laptop and scripts for the upcoming workshop.

I did a quick scan of the businesswoman's newspaper. The column headlines revealed that we live in a time of extremes. On the one hand, we have the overarching embrace of Western civilization, with all its glittering gadgets and staggering achievements enabled by a high-tech worldwide communication system unlike anything ever seen before. On the other, we have the poor and the disenfranchised, all those human beings who are outside the system, including most of the "third world." As an anthropologist, I know this world well, as I've lived and worked in it for much of my life. I glanced again at the woman next to me and wondered if she had ever seen the world of need up close and personal.

On this particular morning, I was considering these two opposing polarities and something completely unexpected appeared in my mind—the words attributed to Jesus of Nazareth, taken from one of his sermons: "Blessed are the meek, for they shall inherit the earth."

I considered this revolutionary statement, utterly at odds with Western economic theory, and I was very much aware that the meek are not doing well, not well at all. I was also aware that many in the international community consider Americans to be the Romans of our time, as our corporations and our banks backed by our military complex relentlessly despoil and plunder the world. I glanced again at the professional next to me and directed a brief but intense surge of focused attention toward her. No contact. She couldn't feel it, or if she could, she was purposefully ignoring me.

I took a couple of deep breaths, and since I had some time, I intentionally relaxed my body, slipping into a light meditative trance. As I settled, I created a thought-form within my mind of Jesus of Nazareth, producing a culturally determined image of a tall Semitic man with long tied-back shaggy hair, a hawk nose, and a scraggly beard, dressed in period clothing with scuffed worn sandals on his bare brown feet. As I held my focused attention on the mental image, something quite startling occurred. A brilliant curved line of light appeared in the air before me about eight feet above the carpeted floor, a shimmering golden crescent somewhat like the new moon with the points up. Amazed, I watched it widen and open so that light began to spill out of it almost like a waterfall.

I risked a quick glance to my right and to my left. Apparently, nobody else could see it. I refocused on the brilliant field and held my breath, enthralled, as a large bubble of light separated from that curtain of radiance. I directed all of my concentration onto this sphere and watched as it darkened and took on density until it transformed into a human shape, fleshed out with those details I had just conjured up based on my knowledge of the classical world.

My mind was reeling. I was aware that I was practicing what the Tibetans call Deity yoga and from the shamanist perspective Deity Mysticism, a discipline in which I had mentally created a thought-form and then projected it outward. But as the image continued to darken and solidify, surrounded by that shimmering golden curtain, I wasn't sure if I had created it or whether I had summoned it.

I claim nothing, yet I understood with certainty in those moments that I had used my own mind and body to create a bridge across which I may have accessed the oversoul field of some great being to bring him through from the worlds of things hidden. To say I was in awe would be an understatement of vast proportions. There I was in the airport, and I was mind-blown.

For long moments, the spirit simply stood still before me and took in his surroundings. Then he turned and observed me thoughtfully, locking his eyes with mine and holding my attention with his gaze. He was not quite solid, but rather somewhat luminous and almost transparent. Those who have read my book *Visionseeker* will remember that we had made contact before, and as the sense of recognition grew between us, a smile appeared on his face and he opened his hands, turning his palms toward me in greeting.

My body became warm, and light flowed into me like water poured into a bottle. My blood began to sparkle, producing a hissing sound like rushing water in my ears. I felt my heart opening as the vibration of absolute and unconditional love began to permeate my being. During this moment of immanence and enchantment, his smile deepened, crinkling the edges of his dark eyes under his tangled mop of hair. I knew then that he could perceive my opened heart, and he looked so real to me in those moments that I could almost smell him.

Part of me wondered idly if anyone else would notice him. Perhaps in response to my thoughts, he turned his head and glanced at the crowds flowing by us like a river. As my gaze followed his, I wondered if anyone would be receptive to a sermon from a spirit who looked like (and could be) Jesus of Nazareth right here, right now, in the airport. Not very likely, I concluded. Anyone who could see him clothed in what appeared to be several layers of long white homespun bathrobes would immediately wonder how this striking and yet decidedly ungroomed figure ever got by airport security. He continued to scan the crowd, his attention resting on the restless multitudes surging by, and nobody noticed him. Nobody.

Abruptly, his attention shifted to a tired and distraught mother dealing with an upset child nearby, pulling my own focus in her direction as well. My heart was overflowing with love in those moments, and being a father myself, I extended my feelings of compassion toward the mother and her child. Amazingly, the little girl stopped crying, allowing herself to be comforted by her mother. The crisis seemed to be over. The tall spirit glanced at me and nodded with . . . with what? Satisfaction? Approval?

My thinking mind slowly began to operate once again, and as my sense of self restabilized, thoughts appeared. Who was this spirit? Was he my Spirit Guide who had chosen to make an appearance as the thought-form I had created? Was he an angel? Was he an expression of an oversoul field that included the historical Jesus? I focused my attention on the spirit—or the angel (he had no wings)—standing before me as these questions moved through my mind and he simply looked at me and into my soul.

Then he smiled . . . and his image slowly became more and more transparent until all that remained was the large shimmering bubble tinged by a deep bluish purple and surrounded by a radiant outline of light. The sphere faded from my sight as it merged back into that curtain of light that was now flowing back up into the brilliant arc, and then it too disappeared as though someone had closed it from the other side. I was left with the resonance of his smile and the warmth of his eyes. That, for me, was his sermon, his message from the field of good.

As I wiped the tears from my eyes and reviewed what had just happened, I glanced at the woman next to me. She was still studying the stock market page and had noticed nothing. I wondered if she knew anything about shamans. Twenty years ago, I would have said probably not. Today, I could not be so sure. Interest in the shaman's path is growing, and as a shamanist, I know that although such experiences are not exactly commonplace for all of us, they do happen, often unexpectedly, like this one.

As I have already noted, the difference between a shaman and a yogi practicing Deity yoga lies in the yogi's conviction that the deity is simply a thought-form and thus an illusion created by their own mind. A shaman, in contrast, would be equally as convinced that the deity was indeed a spirit with its own separate agenda and being-hood, quite distinct from the one who perceived it. I had not presumed to step forward and merge with the exalted being who had spiritwalked through the gateway created by my mind, yet when I considered the incredible surge of unconditional love I had just experienced, I suspected that he had merged with me.

I continued to sit in my airport seat and marvel at the wonder of it. Then the moment passed as my flight was announced and I rose to shuffle onto the plane with the others. I noted in passing that the businesswoman was in first class. I was flying coach. I stowed my gear in the overhead compartment above my seat and dug out a book to read while we rode the winds to our distant destination.

The Pagan Christ

I was thinking about this extraordinary encounter upon awakening at 4:00 a.m. one day. I lay still in the darkness, watching my thoughts, and after the usual suspects had passed through my mind, I suddenly wondered how many of our religious specialists—our rabbis, priests, ministers, and imams—have had visionary revelations themselves or have made important discoveries through their theological or historical research. And for those who have, I wondered further, how do they manage to incorporate their revelations into their teachings to enlighten their spiritual communities? Here's an interesting example from one who has experienced both, one who chose, like me, to publish.

In 2004, Tom Harpur, a Canadian theologian and Anglican priest, published a book titled *The Pagan Christ: Recovering the Lost Light*. His discourse begins with his revelation that Isis, the ancient Egyptian goddess of love and the archetypal mother, had a second name, a nickname, four thousand years ago—Mery, which means "beloved" in the Egyptian language. And her son Horus, immaculately conceived after the death of his father, the god Osiris, had a second name too—Iusa.[12] Sound familiar?

Grounded in relentless scholarship, perhaps encouraged by spiritual insight, Harpur's book reveals that the Christos myth was alive and well in Egypt more than two thousand years before the story of Jesus of Nazareth appeared in the Middle East. And his discovery? The Egyptian god Horus was and is the pagan Christ. Harper documents how his myth was "borrowed" part and parcel from the Egyptian mystery schools by the early Christian theologians who then created a figurative flesh-and-blood Jesus—an embodied god-human hybrid on earth for the common people to believe in as the son of God and a divine messiah and redeemer.[13]

Harpur describes this blatantly political act as "the shadow of the Third Century" because once the Christian church had taken the Christos myth from the Egyptians and made it their own, they did everything they could to destroy any evidence of their mythos's pagan roots.[14] In *Not in His Image*, John Lamb Lash writes that this included the systematic destruction of the Egyptian and Greek mystery schools as well as the extermination of the Gnostics who called themselves *telestai* (those who are aimed). The telestai were the university professors and wisdom keepers of the ancient world for more than a thousand years.[15]

Lash reveals that the Gnostics' practice of telestics was the art of interpreting the mystical and supernatural elements of human experience in a sober and rational manner but without dismissing or denying the authenticity of such experience.[16] Gnosis itself was an ancient form of noetics, the science of relating mind to phenomena through direct experience, natural and supernatural. In telestics, the insights of noetic science can be brought to focus specifically on issues of human purpose, cosmic order, and so forth. Fortunately, some of the Gnostics' wisdom survived by chance in the fourth-century Nag Hammadi scriptures recovered from a cave in Egypt in 1945. Lash has summarized much of this knowledge.

There are parts of Harpur's book that some readers may find challenging, such as his conclusion that it is questionable, even doubtful, that a flesh-and-blood Jesus ever lived. He suggests that the entire story of Jesus, from his immaculate conception right up to his sacrifice and his resurrection, was completely fictional and was a reworking of the myth of Horus of Egypt.

Harpur is not alone in his assertions. In fact, the list of scholars, historians, and independent researchers who have detailed evidence that it is unlikely that Jesus ever existed is extensive. For example, Acharya S, writing under the pen name D. M. Murdock, goes into great detail in her book *Christ in Egypt: The Horus-Jesus Connection* about the stunning similarities between Jesus and the ancient Egyptian god Horus. The sources she cites are anything but marginal or questionable and are entirely within the mainstream of Egyptology.[17] Her books *The Christ Conspiracy: The Greatest Story Ever Sold* and *Suns of God: Krishna, Buddha, and Christ Unveiled* examine Jesus as a deity fabricated by ancient people as a personification of the sun.[18] She maintains that Jesus did not, in fact, exist as a person but only as a myth and an idea.

In addition, Michael Paulkovich, a biblical historian, has come forward with the book *No Meek Messiah: Christianity's Lies, Laws, and Legacy*, which suggests that Christ was a myth fabricated by the gospel writers.[19] To come to this conclusion, Paulkovich examined the writings of 126 ancient historians who he says should have mentioned Jesus in their documents. In fact, no ancient historian mentions Jesus at all. Paulkovich's research was originally published in the journal *Free Inquiry*, and in it, Paulkovich claims that the only mention of Jesus comes from the Bible itself.

Many additional historians have written numerous books making the same claim. Joseph Atwill, a biblical scholar, has posited that the myth of Jesus was fabricated to unite the Roman kingdom under a singular leader—Constantine. His book, *Caesar's Messiah: The Roman Conspiracy to Invent Jesus*, details his claims.[20] John G. Jackson's *Pagan Origins of the Christ Myth* explores how ancient pagan religions are reflected in the Jesus myth.[21] There are numerous identical stories that exist in paganism and the gospels, such as the miracle of a deity changing water into wine. Countless scholars and historians have noted the parallels between the story of Jesus and earlier gods. There are many deities who were born of a virgin, for example, and many who performed miracles identical to those of Jesus.

Yet what about all those who have had visionary connections or near-death experiences in which they encountered a being they believed to be Jesus, including my lady Jill's encounter in the chapel in Minnesota? I myself have had a transpersonal connection with a being I interpreted as Jesus of Nazareth, which is recorded in my book *Visionseeker* and in the account detailed above.

As mentioned earlier in this chapter, when Spirit Guides choose to reveal themselves to us, they may often appear to us as figures in our faith—a Christian seeing Jesus, a Jew meeting with Moses, a Muslim encountering the prophet Mohammed, a Hindu encountering Krishna, a Tibetan Buddhist merging with Avalokiteshvara, a Taoist chatting with an immortal who resembles Lao-Tzu. It is also possible that the "Jesus icon" may be an expression of one of the higher organizing intelligences in service to humanity who chooses this symbolic form to make an impression. Could it be that the impression Jill had of Jesus was, in fact, the Spirit Guide of that little boy who took that form to be of service to him? Or was it perhaps an expression of an oversoul field that incarnated as Yeshua Ben Josephus two millennia ago? We must be open to the possibility that the Jesus myth, which took form in the third century, may have been based upon dim memories of a charismatic rabbi who came to a bad end at the hands of the Romans, a man who was a shaman in every sense, a man who could communicate with spirits, journey to the other worlds, and perform miracles. Such personages exist in the Judaic tradition and are known as the Ba'al Shem, the Master of the Name.[22]

HUMANITY DIVINITIZED

Harpur also reveals something in his book that converges directly upon the New Mysteries reappearing in our time. He presents us with a central teaching found at the heart of all the world's religions and in every culture—the incarnation of the divine into human form. This is familiar territory in Christianity, in which this teaching takes the form of Jesus being the son of God. Yet in considering the nature of divinity, Harpur observes that the solar being we call the sun is the Source and thus the actual creator of everything in our solar system.[23] For example, all the carbon in our body (as a carbon-based life-form) was forged at the heart of our star. It is also by its light alone that we are able to know and see everything that exists. Therefore, Harpur posits, the sun was a natural symbol in antiquity for the ultimate Source of all being, for God.

This divine Source of all life was mythically manifested across time in countless accounts as the radiant figure of the humanized sun god, a symbolic representative of both the divine and also humanity divinitized. Such solarized beings included Apollo in Greece, Horus in Egypt, Mithras among the Persians, Jesus of Nazareth of the Middle East, and others. The list is long and through the myths and stories about these archetypal heroes, humankind could see pictured their own history, their own destiny to become heroes themselves, and their own eventual conversion (ascension) to become godlike beings of light. Seen in this perspective, each of us is an embodied seed of soul light sourced into us by our oversoul, who is, in fact, a being of light. This reveals that each one of us is a son or a daughter of God and that each of us is a manifestation of the light of our oversoul, our god-self embodied.

Harpur also reiterates a fact well known to mythologists: myths such as those that make up much of the Bible were never intended to be taken as factual.[24] Myths are fictions; they are traditional symbolic stories dealing with supernatural beings, ancestors, or heroes that inform and shape the worldview of a people. Yet every myth and every fairy tale embodies timeless truths that are real. These myths are not to be taken literally; they are meant to be understood. Even children can understand that they are not literal.

AN ETERNAL TRUTH

The myths that gave rise to our Judeo-Christian-Islamic religious traditions, correctly understood, contain an extraordinarily important eternal truth: the divine seed of light sourced into us by our personal god, our immortal oversoul, with our first breath at the beginning of our life, is the true Christos.

From my personal experiences and my own research, I know that the mystics of antiquity taught their acolytes that we received our divine seed of light when we took our first breath, revealing that the breath is the link between spirit and form. We have already observed that all three of our Abrahamic traditions agree that God breathes life into form.

We discover through spiritual vision that the teachers of the ancient mystery schools knew that this "God" is actually our own immortal spirit soul who breathes life into us. In the philosophy of Aristotle, the oversoul was known as our "entelechy" (en-TELL-e-key), our personal spiritual essence—which is already fully realized—and our immortal vital force, which continually directs us toward self-fulfillment, the condition under which a potential becomes actualized. Aristotle also understood the oversoul/entelechy to be the vital principle that guides the development and functioning of an organism. This truth, correctly understood, reveals that the Christos, known by many names in many cultures, is present within every single member of humanity as our common spiritual property.

Through our own personal visionary experience, we come to know with certainty that the accepting and embracing of this extraordinary revelation, the power of the Christos within each of us, may be activated and unleashed to spiritualize our own nature. The Gnostics taught that through direct experience (gnosis) of the sacred nature of our entelechy and its soul seed within us, we discover that each of us embodies a part of the Originator and that the presence of the Christos within us gifts each one of us with the potential to become gods ourselves.

Blasphemy? Absolutely not, and yet virtually none of our monotheistic Abrahamic traditions affirms this progression. But the Eastern Orthodox Christian tradition does.

The Eastern Orthodoxy and Saint Symeon

While the Western Catholic Church in Rome has placed more and more power in the hands of its pope, cardinals, and bishops over the past seventeen hundred years, the guardians of spiritual truth in the Eastern Orthodoxy are considered to be the entire people of God—the populace at large. This has created a strongly democratic religious complex in the Eastern Christian world about which most in the West are largely unaware.

When I was traveling in Greece many years ago, I came across a book by Patricia Storace titled *Dinner with Persephone: Travels in Greece*. I was struck by this passage about the Eastern Orthodoxy:

> Our people have followed the path that Alexander laid down for us in the pre-Christian world and Constantine in the fulfilled world—[the goal] of becoming gods. This is part of our Orthodox theology, not like your "salvation" [in the Western tradition], which puts a piece of virtue in the bank and gets back divine grace as interest. To understand us, you must understand the concept of theosis [becoming one with God]. Our [Eastern] church teaches that the goal of each Christian is deification [to become God]—Saint Athanasius wrote that the Christ says to us, "In my kingdom, I shall be God with you as gods."[25]

To merge with and become one with God—now, that is a truly great adventure, don't you think? And in the shamanist tradition, the merging and becoming one with our god-self is available to all of us and all the time, no matter what one's spiritual beliefs or religion may be.

My favorite saint in the Eastern Orthodox tradition is a tenth-century monk who was born with the Christian name George and eventually canonized as Saint Symeon (949–1022). My Internet searches have revealed that he was one of only three given the title "New Theologian" by the church. The word *theologian* in the perspective of those times meant "one who has had the direct one-on-one mystical experience of God."

Saint Symeon achieved his transpersonal connection with what he perceived as the light of the "Holy Spirit" through dedicating his life to the practice of *hesychia* (HESS-ick-ia)—the cultivation of a stillness or silence of the heart. Hesychia is a form of meditation that incorporates directed inner focus and control of the breath with an intention, usually expressed through prayer. This is a mystical practice much like that of the deep listening of some of the Australian Aboriginals called dadirri, which Sandra Ingerman and I described in *Awakening to the Spirit World.* This similarity reveals that the traditional peoples knew about this and practiced it as well. Symeon encouraged all Christians in his writings and teachings to have the direct experience of God in deep contemplation through hesychia. In one of his discourses, he defended his frequent sharing of his own inner experiences, writing that it was not presumptuous but was done to encourage others in their inner life.[26]

Through the discipline of hesychia, Saint Symeon and his acolytes (his hesychasts) attained visions of divine light through intentionally breathing into their hearts where they activated and merged with the Christos seed residing within it. This is authentic Deity Mysticism in every sense, a practice that will bring the spiritual seeker into direct conscious relationship with their immortal oversoul, their god-self.

Saint Symeon perceived the visionary life to be quite ordinary. He understood that to achieve the direct, transpersonal connection with that field of grace that he called the Holy Spirit is one of our natural birthrights, as I too have suggested. He is reputed to have said that only those who become aware of signs and wonders happening within themselves are truly God-bearers.[27]

A thousand years later, his insights confirm that any authentic spiritual practice or religion worth its salt must be about helping us achieve that direct connection with the sacred light that dwells within our hearts—the Christos seed that we received from our oversoul when we drew our first breath. Saint Symeon reveals, as have countless mystics across time, that it is through the experience of connecting directly with our oversoul that each of us can access the greater spiritual "god-field" of the human spirit in the Upper Worlds. This is a spiritual collective composed of all the human higher selves pooled into one vast holographic mosaic, one that contains within itself the composite wisdom and experience of our species that is known in many mystical traditions as the Akashic Records and that Jung knew as the collective unconscious. The Hawaiian kahuna mystics like Hale Makua called it Ka Poʻe ʻAumakua, the great gathering, or field, of the human oversouls. We might simply think of it as "the human spirit," of which each one of us is a manifested expression.

This is why Saint Symeon and countless other mystics have counseled that the answers to all the mysteries lie within us, answers that can be accessed through the practice of deep listening through the stillness of our heart. He knew that through this inner meditative silence, it was possible to become one with God—to actually become God—an awareness that lies outside the teachings of the Western church yet is very much part of the New Mysteries coming into being in our time.

Unification

The growing acceptance of this truth, the possibility for us to become God, has enormous implications, for it carries the potential to unify all three of our Abrahamic religious traditions—Judaism, Christianity, and Islam—into one singular, spiritual complex.

When this unification occurs, our world will change dramatically and for the better. Our understanding and acceptance that all of our Judeo-Christian-Islamic teachings are manifestations of a single, central theme will enable each of us to acquire both the power and the responsibility to become our own prophet, our own teacher, receiving our own mystical revelations from the highest spiritual sources ourselves, without the need for any mythic father-god, bureaucratic priesthood, or salvationist redeemer complex standing between us and our experience of the divine.

Does this mean that we have to abandon our churches and temples, zendos and mosques? Of course not. These are the centers of our spiritual communities and the source of much comfort and support. However, we might consider taking these thoughts into those communities for meditation and discussion. The time has come for us to live our lives and behave toward each other as though we are embodied Gods in training. And now that you know this, it is very difficult to unknow it. As I have already mentioned, the time has definitely come for an upgrade!

THE NEW DIRECTION

In opposition to humanity's current self-serving and self-destructive dominator scenarios, our involvement with the New Mysteries encourages a return to the nature-revering spirituality of our ancestors, one that will lead us toward a reconnection with the world soul. The shamanist persuasion enables a new level of connection with the great mystery of life because that is where the mystic road begins.

In my own practice, I continue to explore what's possible through my journeywork. Once in relationship with the hidden worlds, each of us may receive revelations and teachings directly from our inner sources of wisdom and power. These include our helping spirits, our personal oversoul, our Spirit Guide, as well as the world soul herself.

A NEW FOUNDATION

The awareness that we can achieve such connections with the sacred central intelligence agency (SCIA) of the earth, of nature, stands at the epicenter of the New Mysteries. It is an integral part of our re-enchantment, one that may convey to us the knowledge and certainty of our ecological niche, our job description within Sophia's dream (see chapter 3). Only this, in my humble opinion, will reveal to us the current shape and direction of our destiny as souls traveling across time. And only this may encourage us to behave in ways to soften the environmental catastrophe that now seems to be on final approach.

In thinking about what has been from my perspective as a pre-historian, and in contemplating the various possibilities of what's coming into being from my perspective as a shamanist, several givens come up for consideration. For example, we are living in a time of great change, with things coming apart. This is also a time in which increasing numbers of spiritual seekers are leaving our mainstream religions. Yet as I have indicated, this is not an atheistic movement.

Given the number of websites and workshops devoted to exploring different aspects of spirituality and the unending avalanches of well-intentioned books written on these and related subjects during the past several decades, an interesting possibility now arises.

Among the shamans of the traditional peoples, it was always understood that each new generation across time had the responsibility to perpetuate and refresh a continuously re-created tradition—even adding to and changing the accumulating horde of spiritual treasures—as they made it their own. For it was always in this way that this ancient visionary road remained both vital and meaningful to those who were walking it.

With the ending of this cycle, we now have the same sacred responsibility that our ancestors carried. To act on this will require courage as well as the willingness to bless and let go of anything—religious or otherwise—that is outdated and no longer serves us. This is about shedding burdens. And at the same time, this is not just about the deconstruction of what was. It is also about the building of what is coming into being. It's about the creation of a new spiritual foundation, a new worldview, a new cultural mythos, a new story. This deserves our full attention.

MAX ZELLER'S DREAM

Toward the end of the 1940s, the esteemed psychologist Carl Jung had a conversation with his friend Max Zeller who told him about a recurrent dream he had been having.[1] In the dream, Zeller saw uncountable numbers of people, and of every race and culture, working on what appeared to be the foundation of an immense temple. As far as he could see, all the way to the horizon and in all directions, swarms of people appeared to be raising an endless number of great stone pillars; in fact, Zeller himself was one of those engaged in this huge task within his dream.

When he asked Jung if he knew the meaning of the dream, Jung responded that he did. When queried further, Jung said the great temple was the new religion coming into being and that vast numbers of people were already actively involved in its construction.

Zeller then asked Jung how he knew this to be so, to which the psychologist responded that many of his clients had reported having the same dream and that he himself had had it. When Zeller then asked Jung how long he thought it would take to create this new religion, Jung told him "six hundred years" with a twinkle.

Six hundred years—it was approximately this span of time required to formalize and codify the new religion of early Christianity that supposedly began within a Judean splinter group called the Zaddikim during the Roman period in Judea and then expanded dramatically in response to the Roman emperor Constantine's conversion in the fourth century. Backed by the military might of the Roman Empire, Christianity came to dominate our current age for the next seventeen hundred years, and from that time to the present, the popes became (and still are) the emperors of Rome.

THE CYCLE OF AGES AND A NEW RELIGION

In *Awakening to the Spirit World*, I wrote about the four stages through which we have passed during the great cycle of ages just completed, a cycle that lasted for perhaps twenty-six thousand years. The first stage was the late Stone Age, a period that extended from perhaps 26,000 to 12,000 BCE in which humanity was still engaged in hunting and gathering as a lifeway. The second stage was the Mesolithic-Neolithic period, which extended from 12,000 to 4000 BCE, heralding the beginnings of agriculture and settled communities. The third stage could be called the classical period, which included the rise of civilization states extending from the Sumerians around 5000 BCE to the end of the Roman period. The fourth stage has lasted from the rise of Christianity in the fourth century CE to the present, a span of about seventeen hundred years.

In the first stage, the dominant spiritual practice was sha-manism—nature-focused spirituality. In the second, it was shamanism plus the awareness of nature as personified as the great goddess, perhaps; we don't really know, but we begin to find small portable images of women rendered in stone and ivory and ceramic with increasing frequency. In the third stage, polytheism appears in association with the first state-level societ-ies accompanied by the belief in many high gods and goddesses above nature. And in the fourth stage, monotheism emerges, a form of polytheism with many deified saints and sages but with a supernatural emperor, father-god, or CEO on top. In other words, with each stage a new religion came into being, and as our perceptions of ourselves and our societies became more complex, more stratified, and more centralized, so did our collective mythos about the supernatural realms. The same thing is happening now.

We are now at the beginning of the next cycle of ages, and the attentions of a substantial portion of our population have turned toward spirituality as reflected in the plethora of books and workshops on mysticism, shamanism, Buddhism, mindfulness meditation, Zen, Taoism, Kabbala, Sufism, and Gnosticism. Then there is the avalanche of books and workshops on self-awareness, personal development, and finding our soul's purpose, which reveal that more and more of us are growing beyond our old belief systems and the religions in which we were raised and are embracing a more expanded version of ourselves, as well as who and what we are becoming in a new way. In drawing upon all these resources, it does seem that a new kind of religion or spiritual complex is quietly taking form.

Increasing numbers of us are searching for enhanced self-awareness on the one hand and reconnection with the archetypes that our visionary ancestors sought out across time on the other—with those authentic transpersonal beings who are poised and willing to help us and who always seem to want the best for us. This impulse seems to be part of a progression forward and upward toward the new spiritual complex. This may be the new religion described by Jung at whose center can be found that cluster of core beliefs held by the transformational community. I have written about these in my other books and will add a few more points here.

The mysteries in every age have always begun with the adventure of self-discovery—with the quest to find out who and what we really are, where we came from, and what our purpose for being here is. It has always been through this quest that we have acquired an enhanced awareness of what our life lessons are, the ones on which we are currently working and the ones that reveal our path through this life.

As we progress in our quest, the process is much like peeling an onion, whereby we remove those outer layers that we took on unconsciously from our families and friends and from society at large—those social values and beliefs and morals about who we think we are (or should be), as well as who we are afraid we are (or not). As we peel them away, we find within our essential self the lost light of our true spiritual nature, which usually has nothing whatsoever to do with the script that most of us were handed at birth by our parents and by the culture or the religion in which we were raised.

Connection with our authentic inner oversoul seed of light provides us with a greater understanding of who and what we really are, and yet as we discover this, we learn that we must also practice discernment as to how much of our new awareness can interface with that of our families and friends, as well as with society at large. For it is not in alignment with the visionary path to create disharmony or discord, although this does sometimes happen.

The kahuna Hale Makua observed often that the first question we must address is, who are we? This brings us to return to the discussion in chapter 6 on the three souls that come together to create the self. It is of interest that in Buddhism's central doctrines, now very popular in the West, the self is often proclaimed to be an illusion. From the perspective of the Polynesian kahuna mystics and many other indigenous peoples, this proclamation is in deep error. There is indeed a self that we develop in each life. In fact, there are two selves, our higher spiritual "overself" that resides forever in the dreaming, and our physically manifested earthly self here. And it is through this dual vehicle of the two selves that we as immortals travel across time.

And why is this correction so important? Because in order to experience authentic initiation, to become who and what you are to become as an authentic being in life, you have to know who you are. And your dual-natured self is most definitely not an illusion.

The Path that Only We Walk On

When we step onto our path—the path that only we walk on—the New Mysteries beckon, inviting us into the deeper levels of wisdom where we may learn much about the nature of reality and how this interfaces with the nature of ourselves.

In my experience as a scientist and a shamanist, this wisdom cannot be acquired from belief systems or scripture, nor can it be gleaned from faith alone. It must be derived from the direct connection with the transpersonal worlds that are all around us as well as within us. For as Saint Symeon and Hale Makua knew, this experience alone conveys upon us the mantle of authentic initiation. As we receive this mantle, everything changes. Through meditative shamanist journeywork, the spiritual seeker may experience the great field of power that underlies and infuses everything everywhere with life force, a field of which your own soul complex is an expression. As I have mentioned, the life force is continually emanated by the Originator, whose profound accomplishment at the universal level is the transformation of inorganic energy and matter into organic life, ultimately leading to the evolution of sentient (self-aware) life forms that eventually transmute themselves to become godlike beings who step up and into the spiritual hierarchy.

This is the purpose of the universes, and we are all going in this direction. At the end of our evolution as souls, we will merge once again with the Source, which will incorporate into itself the gifts of everything that we have done and become during our long journey across time. It is in this manner that the Originator grows, increases, and becomes more as it travels across eternity. And eternity is a long time.

This is a central theme in this book, and it is my hope that my field reports will enhance your own visionary investigations, encouraging you to go where few embodied souls have gone before.

Another central theme reveals that the visionaries of the old mystery schools knew that the great field of living light—the great central sun, which is the Source, the Originator—is impersonal and remote, and yet their experience has shown that when conditions are favorable, this field can and does respond in subtle ways, giving us that "one taste" that the philosopher Ken Wilber has described in his book *One Taste: Daily Reflections on Integral Spirituality*.[2] Insights such as these can completely change the one who receives them, and as we are transformed, so is the world. This gives us something to look forward to, wouldn't you agree? And if personal transformation is what you are searching for, sooner or later it will catch up with you and find you.

Through the consciousness of the millions of spiritual seekers at large in our time, the new religious complex that Max Zeller and Carl Jung talked about more than sixty years ago is quietly taking form, one that will likely replace or at the least considerably change our current mainstream religious traditions. And given our sophisticated and global systems of communication, this may happen in considerably less than six hundred years.

The New Mysteries now ask us an all-important question: How is each of us to define our own personal standard of humanity? In searching for answers, we have the potential to achieve a higher value. The word *value* in this sense refers to our attitudes that inform and mold our behaviors. And it is precisely here that our behaviors may embrace the foundation stone of Indigenous Mind—respect—rather than the foundation stone of the Western world—domination—and this is worth considering.

Within the transformational community, increasing numbers of people seem to be concerned with the quality of life at all levels of society, and human relationships are perceived as more important than personal gain. This awareness reveals that the new spiritual complex coming into being has a deeply humanistic focus at its center, one that is giving rise in our time to a new form of mystical humanism, one in which the old divisions between liberal and conservative, between Jew and Christian and Muslim, between Buddhist and Hindu, or between conservative patriot and progressive liberal become transparent.

I personally find this perspective to be deeply reassuring, as being a humanist has everything to do with being a progressive in the evolved sense of those words. Although the Western world continues to be driven by greed and fueled by denial, motivated by fear, and dominated by competition, members of the transformational community are oriented toward democratic, humanistic ideals, and we tend to favor cooperative endeavors that benefit the many.

The importance of balance and harmony lies right at the core of our values, and in this respect, we, like the indigenous peoples, have grasped that humans must strive to live their lives in ways that contribute to the greater good of all rather than following lifestyles and pursuing goals that create its opposite.

The time has come for all of us, including our leadership, to turn toward our higher nature, to bring out the best in ourselves in order to lift our anchor out of the negative polarity and re-sink it into the positive so that we may work together to create connection and community with an enhanced sense of purpose and mutual cooperation.

To quote a Hawaiian saying, "We are all in the canoe together, and if we keep paddling in the right direction and we keep bailing, we'll reach the island."

A Humanist Perspective

At the moment that we achieve this level of awareness, we step up to be in service to our colleagues, friends, and family members, and even humanity at large, all those who are still entrapped in samsara—the world of illusion—assisting them so that they may ascend to the next level in their own personal evolution as souls traveling across eternity. However, this is not about missionizing the unready and the unwilling. It is not our job to inflict self-realization upon others, because it simply doesn't work that way. The experience unfolds in layers for those who are prepared, for those heroes who are ready, willing, and able to assume the chase.

Hale Makua was fond of observing that in the positive polarity, the practice of the priest, the shaman, the mystic, or the healer is and forever will be about compassionate action, thought, feeling, speech, and relationship with the other, whoever and whatever the other might be. No judgment. It is only in the positive polarity, not the negative, that the spiritual teacher or practitioner can be a healer or a teacher by example, and thus a world redeemer. This is the bodhisattva path on which exalted souls walk—those who have completed their evolutionary cycle of embodiments and who are ready to step up and into the spiritual hierarchy but who choose to postpone their own "nirvana" so that they may return again and again, coming back into this world of pain and suffering to be of service to all those still stuck in their stuff. In addition, Makua said often that it is only when we are in the positive polarity that it becomes possible to connect with our helping spirits, our spirit teachers, our Guide, and our ancestors.

Makua also gently observed that the negative polarity of the priest or priestess, the missionary or healer, is zeal. The negative polarity is not necessarily bad, although it certainly can be. When we are in the negative polarity, we discover that nothing can be accomplished on behalf of others or ourselves. Yet this is where we often learn our lessons.

THE MASTERS OF DECEPTION

In chapter 7, I discussed the far-reaching impacts of the negative polarity. We must now consider one of the great theological questions that humanity has pondered over the millennia: Why would a benevolent father-god allow evil to play such an enormous role in our world? On planet Earth today, evil exists at all levels, from domestic violence and public shootings to political, economic, military, and religious terrorism. The root causes of evil need to be clearly understood, for only when we comprehend the true nature of what we're dealing with can we transcend and resolve the distortions in our world, as well as those that lurk within our own character. And for those who proclaim with fervor that there is no such thing as "evil," this is a very nice theory. Unfortunately, it is in error.

THE EGREGORES

Many years ago, I was reading an anonymously written essay on the Internet and came across a term that was unfamiliar to me: *egregore*. I journeyed toward my spirit teacher (my oversoul) at this point to ask for information, and this is what I received:

An egregore is a nonmaterial psychic entity, or minded energetic field, uniting members of a group or organization (a religion or state, a corporation or political party, an association or cult, for example) generated and maintained by the thought energy (belief systems) of the group members.

Such an entity can, in turn, influence the individuals, as well as the collective psyche of the group members, taking on a life of its own that may persist even when the original members of the group leave or pass on. The words *psychic entity* and *energetic field* reveal that an egregore is not a true spirit. In fact, it's not a spirit at all. Rather, egregores are dense collective thought-forms that have been created by humans and that owe their continued existence to the mental focus of their believers. They do not live in the dreaming of the spirit world but rather reside in the mental-emotional-psychic realms of the human mind as dark and uninvited guests.

The transmission went on to define an egregore as an entity that resides within us as a mind parasite that can be especially powerful within groups or individuals that it "rides." Addicts, for example, know it as "the monkey on my back." Such egregores are everywhere today, and it is they who embody the dark forces that distract us, confuse us, and keep us from discovering who we are and what we are really supposed to be doing here. They are the "dark ones."

From this information, I suddenly understood that there is an egregore astride our Western society, a mind parasite that may be one of the seed children of ancient Rome whose organized hierarchical social order and legalistic rules enforced by the Roman military machine were and are designed to support the lords of finance, political power, and religion. Sound familiar? Their rules were and are designed to enslave us financially, politically, spiritually, mentally, and emotionally, and this has been going on since the emperor Constantine's conversion seventeen hundred years ago! I understand now that they are still very much in place in our world today!

In dialogue with my teacher and my guide, I learned that these egregores also oppose the reunification of our soul seed with its eternal spirit form, our oversoul, in the afterlife, and the egregores accomplish this by encouraging us to create false belief systems of a hypothetically blissful and exclusive afterlife place called Heaven or Paradise, which only some get to go to while others do not. This is the classic divide-and-conquer scenario: the in-group (our guys) versus the out-group (those guys), and with little effort we can see how this strategy creates separation, which translates into all levels of our society: socially, politically, economically, and spiritually.

Through the shamanic path of direct revelation, we discover that these alleged postmortem Heavens are illusions—thought-forms that have been encouraged by egregores and then created by human beings through the collective imagination of various religious groups—places that exist in the transitional Middle Worlds of dreams between life here on earth and the true afterlife among the higher spheres of the Upper Worlds. These illusory Heavens are traps of considerable proportion in which transiting souls are ensnared so that they never return to resume a relationship with their oversoul between lives.

The transmission concluded by describing how these egregores continually try to inhibit us from manifesting the New Mysteries for the benefit of all humanity, and how virtually all our modern social, political, economic, military, and religious institutions include egregores as psychic-energetic attachments that are essentially running the show at all levels.

The 'E'epa

I spoke with the Hawaiian elder Hale Makua about these egregores years ago. His response is recorded in the final chapter of *The Bowl of Light* in which he called them by their Hawaiian name, *'e'epa*, and revealed them to be "free-ranging psychic entities, invisible beings who function as mind parasites and who prey on those susceptible to their influence."[1] He described them as interdimensional demons who are devious and whose motivation is deception. He confirmed that they are not true spirits, and that psychics who channel are particularly vulnerable to them because these deceivers reside in the same realm in which most psychics operate—the mental-emotional-psychic levels of awareness and experience that are quite separate from the spirit worlds of the dreaming beyond them.

Makua conveyed to me that the masters of deception are accomplished shape-shifters who are good at mimicking and who can assume forms meaningful to those they choose to deceive. They can simply pluck these forms out of the mind of the person to whom they are attached, then appear to them in that way, telling them exactly what they want to hear. Unless psychics are adept at checking their sources, it is very easy for them, or anyone else for that matter, to be deceived.

The Archons

John Lamb Lash has discussed the Gnostic perception of these entities in his book *Not in His Image*, revealing them as the masters of deception who the Gnostics called the "archons," beings that exist as "delusional nodes" in the human mind, quasi-autonomous psychic entities, cosmic imposters, and parasites who pose as gods but who lack the diverse factor of creative will.[2]

According to the Gnostics, the archons cannot originate or create anything; they are not nor have they ever been creators, though they claim to be. They can only imitate, and they operate through psychic stealth. The Gnostics perceived them as invasive, and unlike the divine Aeons who create without imposing themselves, the archons wrongly believe that they can impress their mentality and their intentionality upon humanity. They want to make themselves like us, but they are constantly foiled by the superiority of the human species, which possesses free will and the capacity for creative imagination. The archons do not possess these abilities. They exist here on planet Earth as an alien life form.

Lash reveals that the Gnostic writings in the Nag Hammadi texts consistently stress that humanity is superior to the archons, yet when our faculty of discernment (a function of our egoic mental soul) is weak, we are prone to let pretense and fantasy overwhelm clear thinking.[3] Under this situation, we risk being deviated by another kind of mind, the artificial and alien intelligence of the archons. Lash reveals that from the Gnostic perception, the Judeo-Christian religion was infected right from its inception by the delusional beliefs of this alien mindset.[4]

The Gnostics called the Judeo-Christian alleged father-god the "Demiurge" and revealed it as the lord archon, the arch deceiver. They perceived the Christian god as a demented and insane entity, whose real name is Yaldabaoth, one who has been working against humanity as an adversary from the very beginning. The Gnostics further taught that the true way for humanity could be found only in refuting and rejecting the archontic beliefs and values imposed on us by the deceivers. As you can imagine, the early Christians in the fourth century didn't appreciate this perspective, and history affirms that the Gnostic wisdom keepers were exterminated by the Christians in a very short period of time.[5]

THE WETIKO

The Jungian analyst Paul Levy has written a powerful book about the deceivers titled *Dispelling Wetiko: Breaking the Curse of Evil*.[6] His entire book is an exploration of our "inhumanity" and how we all participate in it, sometimes intentionally yet often inadvertently. Levy calls the collective psychosis under which we labor *wetiko*, a Cree Indian term that refers to a diabolically wicked person or psychic entity or archontic complex whose nature is demonic and who negatively influences and terrorizes others. His work leads us through the manifestation of wetiko in our culture, our media, our economy, our leadership, our religions, and most important, through ourselves. Levy describes the wetiko as "a psycho-spiritual disease of the soul, a parasite of the mind, one that is currently being acted out en masse on the world stage as a collective mental illness of titanic proportions."[7] He compares it to a virus that covertly operates through the unconscious blind spots in the human mind because it is contagious, rendering people oblivious to their own distortions and delusions, and compelling them to act against their own best interests, as well as those of everyone else.

As a shamanic teacher and practitioner, I have been aware of the deceivers for many years and the power that they as attachments may have on their hosts.

Makua added this from his perspective in a conversation with me before his death:

The *'e'epa* encourage their human hosts to go ever deeper into the negative polarity, into the dark side of their personality. As we continue to go there, we reach a point where we can no longer self-correct. It is at this point that we step across a threshold and into the realm of evil, a dark field to which we then contribute through our actions, thoughts, emotions, words, even in our relationships. The 'e'epa especially attach themselves to our political, corporate, and religious leadership, and in all fairness, these worthies are quite unaware of their negative influence.

The masters of deception exist within their own group complex as discarnate entities within the astral planes of the mental, emotional, and psychic levels of experience. They feed off of the negative energy of those they infect to keep themselves going. They have to do this because they are disconnected from the indwelling life force by refusing to abide by what you call the higher organizing intelligences' incarnational principles. They spend their time traveling our world and attaching themselves to humans vulnerable to them, basically using the dark side of the force (negativity) to achieve their means. In the natural course of cosmic events, they will eventually return and be dissolved back into Teave [Makua's Tahitian term for the Originator], and they are being given every chance to learn the error of their ways and to return to seeking the positive polarity so that they too can begin their journey back home. The main problem is that they do not want to go home. They falsely see themselves as gods and they do not intend to submit to the authority of the higher intelligences.

Makua's insights reveal that as long as disillusioned religious believers focus their attention (devotions) on the egregores, these entities are sustained by their attention and over time can become quite powerful by literally feeding on the energy they receive through that focus and diminishing the life force of their supporters. As such, they become psychic vampires imbued and empowered with whatever the belief system that supports them conveys.

As thought-forms, egregores can achieve a wide variety of effects in the minds of humans through which they can, in turn, manifest ever more effects into the physical plane of human existence. And despite Hollywood's efforts to entertain us with vampire films, vampires are not good guys. As we all know from films and stories, vampires cast no shadow nor can they cast a reflection in a mirror. Understood correctly, this means that the vampires do not want to be seen, for once their presence and their nature has been revealed, the game is up and we become invisible to them—literally. (For those interested, Levy's book *Dispelling Wetiko* includes a chapter titled "Wetiko No More.")

In considering history in this light, it is possible that most of the various polytheistic deities of the first hierarchical societies such as Sumeria, Persia, Babylonia, Assyria, Canaan, Phoenicia, Egypt, Greece, and Rome were egregores intentionally invented by the first bureaucratized priesthoods. As collective thought-forms, they were able to maintain their integration as psychic-energetic patterns imbued with the intentions of their creators as long as their followers continued to pay attention to them with rituals and ceremonies, sacrifices and offerings.

In response to this awareness of the nature of created thought-forms defined and projected as gods, many today are reconsidering the true nature of the father-god that we inherited from our Old Testament precursors. The psychologist Carl Jung was among the reconsiderers. His writings reveal deep insights about the father-god as an archetype manifested by and through the human psyche, an archetype that continues to change as we ourselves change and grow in our travels across time. "Whoever knows God has an effect on him," Jung wrote, and when we look at the origins of this god image, we see that this process of transformation extends well back beyond Judaism and the Old Testament for several thousand years until we come to its source.[8]

Many historians and scholars have proposed that the cultural collective known today as the Jews originated as a cluster of Semitic tribes loosely organized into many pastoralist, nomadic groups in the Fertile Crescent of Mesopotamia near the Persian Gulf. Genetic studies show that most Jews bear a common heritage that originates in the Middle East and that they bear a strongest resemblance to the peoples of that region—a common genetic pool dating back four thousand years. In biblical times, speakers of Hebrew (one of a Semitic language complex that included Canaanite, Phoenician, Arabic, and Aramaic) were concentrated in that part of the Roman Empire known as Judea, and Aramaic became the lingua franca of the Fertile Crescent, gradually pushing Akkadian, Hebrew, Phoenician, Canaanite, and several other Semitic languages to extinction, though Hebrew developed a substantial literature in the Torah and the Tanakh.

With my apologies to the Moses myth and the story of the exodus out of Egypt, those who would become known as the Jews are thought by scholars to have migrated into Judea about thirty-five hundred years ago from the southern Mesopotamian region to the east.

It was also from this part of the world that the father-god image came. It appears to have been borrowed initially by these migrating tribes from the Babylonians whose polytheistic religion included an alternately wrathful, alternately beneficent principal god called Marduk. Among the Persians to the north and east, the archetype of the father-god was known as Ormuzd and came to be called Ahuramazda through the teachings of Zoroaster. But if we go back still further, we find that it was among the Sumerians that this archetype originated. Among them he was known as Enlil.

Drawing from my anthropological lecture notes of many years passed, I can share that the Sumerians were the first people we know of who created a stratified polytheistic religion focused on a mythic pantheon of high gods and goddesses above and beyond nature. Among them were the twin brothers Enlil and Enki, who represented the beginnings of our human conception of the cosmic duality. The positive polarity was personified in Enlil, who would eventually morph to become the monotheist deity Marduk, Ahuramazda, Yahweh, Jehovah, Allah, or simply God (liberally shaped as well by the egregore known as Zeus among the Greeks). The negative polarity was vested in Enki, who would be transformed into Ahriman among the Persians, Baal among the Babylonians, Mara among the Buddhists, and into Satan in the Judeo-Christian-Islamic traditions.

In this regard, Satan is an egregore of human invention. Satan is a thought-form, an archon in the Gnostic perception to whom we have assigned all the negativity that exists on this beautiful planet. Over the past five millennia, we could not find it within ourselves to take on any of the responsibility for the evil that has come into being in response to our behavior, and so Satan was created as a myth to absolve us. As he took on density in response to our belief systems that sustain him, he also took on the job of an arch deceiver. Satan is the master of illusion.

From my shamanist experience, the being known as Lucifer does not fall into this category. Although Lucifer has been branded as the "Devil" and demonized as an archetype of evil by our mainstream monotheists, nothing could be further from the truth. Lucifer and Satan are two completely different entities. For starters, Lucifer is not an egregore. Lucifer is a member of the higher organizing intelligences who serves humanity as a threshold guardian. "He" is a group soul composed of many beings—a family, in fact—and taken together, Lucifer's job is to challenge us, to encourage us to experience the negative polarity in all its manifestations, enabling us to pass through that dark field and hopefully find out who we are and what we are not.

Having passed this test, we then turn to embrace our inner light and in the process we discover what and who we really are. This is in keeping with his name: Lucifer, the light bearer. He can be the source of great wisdom for those ready to listen and awaken to their own true nature. In my experience, the Luciferian agenda is ultimately dedicated to the highest good of all by providing us with a catalyst. And what is that catalyst, you might ask? This is something for you to discover. Here's a clue: Lucifer might be called the "master of desire."

The Father-God

And now what about the father-god?

Jung wrote, "Yahweh . . . is an antimony—a totality of inner opposites, and this is the indispensable condition for his tremendous dynamism."[9] Lash has revealed that according to the Gnostic teachings derived from the surviving Nag Hammadi texts, Yahweh started out as a Canaanite thunder god (somewhat like Zeus among the Greeks) who hated trees and who commanded his followers to cut down the sacred groves of the pagans.[10]

During the Roman period, Yahweh's "humanization" culminated in the myth of his incarnation as the half-divine, half-human Christ, the good god embodied, in keeping with the ancient prophesies of a messiah appearing among the Jews (and according to archeologists, Israelite culture grew out of Canaanite culture). This is supported by the first proto-Canaanite texts that date to around 1500 BC, and linguistically, Hebrew is a close relative of both Canaanite and Aramaic (see Numbers 27:16–18 and Deuteronomy 34:9).

Jung did not perceive Yahweh as a benevolent father figure, by the way. Rather, Jung understood this Old Testament "god" as a sort of "personified brutal force . . . an unethical and non-spiritual mind . . . inconsistent enough to exhibit traits of kindness and generosity combined with a violent power drive. It is the picture of a sort of psychic demon and at the same time of a primitive chieftain aggrandized to a colossal size."[11]

Jung's follower Edward Edinger defined an archetype as "a primordial psychic pattern of the collective unconscious that is at the same time a dynamic agency with intentionality," says C. Michael Smith, author of *Jung and Shamanism in Dialogue: Retrieving the Soul/Retrieving the Sacred*.[12] Seen in this perspective, all such archetypes of human creation hover just offstage from our human drama, awaiting their moment to "constellate" within the individual or the collective psyche, catalyzing processes according to their own agendas and programming that may have far-reaching consequences.

In other words, these egregore archetypes who may include both the father-god that exists at the center of our monotheistic religious traditions, as well as his evil twin Satan, seem to represent culturally determined forces that are in actuality products of our human minds. From the Gnostic view, both the father-god and Satan may simply be different sides of the same archon, and if we understand them correctly, it is not difficult to comprehend and identify the motivation behind all the great evils and atrocities committed by humans in the name of their religion and their god.

Although this fact may be upsetting to some conservative religious sects, there is little doubt that these archetypes were and are projections of our own human multileveled psycho-spiritual complex that is both self-determined and self-limited. And by the way, these egregores are not illusions. Once created by us, they are quite real as long as we continue to pay attention to them and believe in them. The time has come for an upgrade in our understanding of the true nature of divinity as outlined in the prior chapters. In this respect, several questions emerge for our consideration:

- Do we hold on with our back teeth to the old egregores and the archaic belief systems and myths, including the scriptures created during the Dark Ages that continue to sustain them? They desperately want us to do that, for without our attention they will cease to exist, literally.

- Do we create new egregores? This is always a possibility and the old ones are waiting in the wings to see what we will do, as many of them are accomplished shape-shifters. As such, they can simply morph into whatever we want them to be and then go on with the show.

- Or do we let egregores all go, thought-forms all, wishing them well as they "transit out" and we turn our attention toward our personal and collective future in a new and more enlightened way through the mystical humanism emerging in our world?

- And are we ready to let go of them? Those old egregores will give us every reason not to. They've been around for thousands of years, and they will always tell you exactly what you want to hear, posing as your friend, feeding your fears in order to ensure their own continued existence.

The fact is that once we see the masters of deception for who and what they are, they are done for and will vanish from the screen as more and more of us simply hit the delete button and cease to pay attention to them. But what will we replace them with? Given the prominence of some form of religion in people's lives virtually everywhere, it is obvious that there exists a great psychological need to believe in something greater than ourselves.

Again, we are now living in a time of great change. It may also be that what people fear most is change. Yet are we open to embrace this fact, and are we willing to re-excavate and rework the authentic mysteries of existence—the ones that begin with direct experiences with Nature Mysticism and progress upward and into authentic Deity Mysticism (see chapter 7)?

Are we ready to open ourselves to an enhanced relationship with our oversoul, our personal god-self, our immortal spirit soul who loves us unconditionally, and with the real archetypes that the mystics have always sought out across time—the light-beings beyond the form, and the formless beyond the lights? For these are the authentic deities imbued with godlike intelligence, the true transcendent and transpersonal forces poised and willing to help us, and they express one emotion only—love. They are and have always been the higher organizing intelligences that many think of as the angelic forces, and unlike the deceivers who are our adversaries, they are on our side, hoping for the best for us always. And from the shamanist perspective, our connection with them is not about worship; it's about relationship.

When we choose to walk the mystical path of the shamanist, we may incorporate the mysteries that are now coming back into being, bringing all that comes with them into the fabric of our lives, inviting the helping spirits and spirit teachers to provide us with their power, protection, support, and wisdom. We may invite them all, including our own oversoul and our Spirit Guide, to take a more active role in our lives, sending us dreams and visions, ideas and guidance, contributing to our spiritual and personal growth and enhancing our lives beyond measure. Prayer is a good way to converse with them, by the way. So is the meditative practice called shamanic journeywork.

When we decide to leave the old egregores behind, this will enable us to ascend toward the luminous horizon of our personal and collective destiny in a completely new way on our long walkabout across eternity. This will lead us toward our experience of re-enchantment and to our eventual ascension to become godlike beings ourselves. Quite an adventure, don't you think?

9

PERSONAL TRANSFORMATION

Spiritual unfolding usually begins with belief systems, often infused into us as children—the magical and mythic beliefs in God or angels, or Jesus as our savior. As we mature, we often discover that these beliefs are at best mental phenomena—cultural thought-forms with strong emotions attached that are only temporarily sustaining, and not much may change in our lives in response to our holding onto them. Many of us then adopt the next stage of spiritual unfolding: faith. Many choose to remain here throughout life, for faith is a great sustainer—in the short term. For some of us, faith may draw us upward and into the third stage: the direct experience of spirit.[1]

This is what happened to me, as recorded in the first chapter of *Spiritwalker*, when I found myself precipitated into a visionary experience in which I had a direct one-on-one experience of a formidable spirit being, and nothing in my training as an anthropologist prepared me for this. And I might add that nothing has been the same ever since.

I discovered in those moments of direct revelation that I had the power to engage in mystical experiences, and through them I could connect and interact with the real archetypes, the transpersonal forces just there on the other side of the mirror. I have mentioned that these forces are energetic in nature, and they may take on a form that is meaningful to the one with whom they wish to come into relationship . . . or . . . they may reveal themselves as they really are—as the light beyond the form, and the formless beyond the light, imbued with a vast and compassionate intelligence.

I have tried to reveal in my writings that the only real and lasting truths are those that are "self-realized." Many have observed that spiritual teachers come and go, offering their versions of truth in lectures and workshops, conferences and books, until they're blue in the face. But these will not become your truths until you have experienced and understood them deep within the core of your being. In my way of understanding, you should never accept something as true just because someone or some book tells you it is so. But when your inner light brightens and you feel that old warm feeling of excitement welling up from somewhere deep within you, an impulse may emerge that says, "Yes! I knew it!" Hold on to that feeling!

As we mature spiritually, we are given more pieces of the puzzle to understand, and we eventually progress through Nature Mysticism upward and into Deity Mysticism through which we enter into communion with the infinite. This awareness draws us into the fourth stage of our spiritual unfolding: personal transformation.

We are talking here about that ego-shattering, mind-expanding, and soul-enhancing experience known in the East as enlightenment or sometimes in the West as becoming god-aware. This is utterly life transforming, as it conveys to us another level of authentic initiation and provides us with knowledge about our own self-nature and the nature of just about everything else. We may then step into a still higher stage of spiritual unfolding, what Saint Symeon described as becoming one with our personal god: theosis.

Direct connection with our oversoul and with our Spirit Guide allows us to experience the subtle and even the causal realms, the higher levels of true Deity Mysticism. This is what waits for us all out there on the trail, and it's not down and backward into outdated and archaic narcissistic belief systems once again. (By the way, the whole born-again phenomenon falls into this category.) It's up the hill.

I have discussed how many of the archetypes, including the father-god embraced by our monotheistic traditions, may represent culturally determined forces that were and are projections of ourselves, revealing that they are self-determined as well as self-limited. This is not to say that all the discarnate beings that are well known to traditional shamans were created by humans. Quite the contrary. The hierarchy of spiritual beings, the elementals, the nature spirits, and other earthbound entities have been here on planet Earth far longer than ourselves. They include the spirits of our ancestors, as well as all those higher spirits already evolved beyond planetary and solar development who may not be earthbound. Included among them are those compassionate forces poised to help us in various ways and usually called angels. Such a one-on-one encounter with them affirms my awareness that the shaman's path enables a life of wonder that is available to all of us with a little training. It also reveals that the spiritual hierarchy of both the Upper and Lower Worlds may respond and come into relationship with us if we invite them to do so, even acting within and through us as archetypal forces. Whether we define these forces as spirits or gods or as archetypes or thought-forms, the shaman's job, practiced across tens of millennia, has always been devoted largely to dealing with them, bringing them into alignment with humanity and ourselves into connection with them. It is in this way they may be of service to us and we to them.

True Transpersonal Awareness

When we have the one-on-one direct experience of spirit, we become aware that one of the traps of New Age spirituality is its equating of magical and mythic belief systems with the true transpersonal experiences of the deep psychic (Nature Mysticism) and the subtle realms (Deity Mysticism). It is one thing to be inspired by listening to a presentation or by reading something uplifting. It is quite another to have a face-to-face encounter with the awesome jolt of these transpersonal forces on their own ground.

This tendency to equate wishful magical and mythic thinking with the true psychic and subtle seems to be a defining characteristic of New Age spirituality. I feel it is important to stop confusing mythological stories with true transpersonal awareness. It is also important for us to understand that the elevation of myth to true transpersonal illumination is not authentic, though it is very much characteristic of countercultural spirituality.

Does this mean that power animals and angels do not exist? Not at all. The fact is that they are quite real, but we have to progress beyond belief and faith in order to encounter them as they really are. This is the power of the shamanist's persuasion because it provides a simple and time-tested system to achieve connection with transcendence and the beings that are waiting for us to connect with them.

I am well aware that the whole issue of contact with transpersonal beings is a problematic one for us Westerners because we do not grow up in a culture in which the connection with spirits is part of our ongoing experience. In fact, many of our fundamentalist religious sects warn (with great righteousness) against having any contact with spirits because they are "evil." This monumental misconception has generated widespread fear in the populace at large that, in turn, has created separation between us and those transpersonal allies who are poised to help us in various ways.

The atheists even deny their existence altogether (again with great righteousness). Despite these many and varied misguided proclamations and pontifications, allow me to observe that the traditional shamans of the indigenous peoples, as well as those of us "moderns" who walk on the path of direct revelation, assert with their/our considerable authority as accomplished visionaries that the spirits, and the realities they inhabit, are real.

Our authority comes not from beliefs (in spirits, angels, spirit guides, and so on), nor does it come from faith (in the existences of spirits, God, or the like). We know their existence to be a fact from our experiences of them. There is simply nothing like the direct revelation of the spirits to awaken us from the consensus slumber of culture at large and bring us into the irreversible vortex of personal transformation (enlightenment)—for this may provide us with a vastly expanded understanding of who we really are, as well as where we are headed.

AN ENCOUNTER IN EGYPT

Thirteen years ago, I visited Egypt for the first time, excited at the opportunity to connect with the transpersonal beings embodied within the great temples and shrines that still exist there. At that time, there was one deity in particular for whom I felt great attraction—the goddess Isis.

I was aware of Isis in a mythic sense—a goddess who was (and is) the wife of the deity Osiris, the lord of the Lower

Worlds. Isis also played a major role in Osiris's resurrection after his betrayal and murder by his evil brother Set. Isis was the one who retrieved Osiris's dismembered parts and reconstituted him. As such, she serves as a symbolic archetype of healing and reconciliation, as well as soul retrieval.

Isis was also the mother of Horus, immaculately conceived after the death of Osiris, and who would ascend to become the sky god of the Pharaohs, whose embodiment was and is the falcon. As such, Isis represents the Great Mother, who with her son Horus served as the source of the Mary and Jesus myth adopted and reworked by the early Christians.

It is enough to say now that during my visit to Egypt in January 2003, I was only mildly interested in this myth. What I was really going for was connection with the transpersonal force that was and is Isis.

On the decidedly warm afternoon of January 8, 2003, our travel group approached the huge temple of the goddess Hathor at Dendara, west of the Nile River in Upper Egypt. On final approach, we could see the temple's massive stone columns in the vast central hall capped by the four faces of Hathor, each facing in one of the four directions.

In a mythic sense, Hathor, the cow-eared goddess of love, was the historically earlier embodiment of this transpersonal feminine force in the old kingdom. Isis came later. In this perspective, Hathor and Isis are actually different attributes of the same transpersonal being. This is why it is often difficult when looking at the temple images to distinguish which goddess is Isis and which is Hathor. The only way of knowing which is which is to read the associated hieroglyph, Isis being represented by the symbol of a three-leveled throne in profile and Hathor by a box (house) with a falcon inside, reflecting her mythic marriage to Horus, the son of Isis.

From the Hawaiian kahuna perspective, Hathor-Isis would be the Egyptian representative of the feminine force of creation whose common name in Hawai'i was Wahine and whose sacred name was 'Uli 'Uli (Uri Uri in Tahitian). I mention this because I have come to understand that these archetypal forces have been perceived in much the same way in all of the world's mystical traditions. For example, I have been told that the Polynesian healer god Lono (once a real man who became a god) became Apollo among the Greeks, Quetzalcoatl among the Aztecs, Kukulkan among the Mayans, Aesclapios among the Greeks, and Imhotep among the Egyptians. Same archetypal force, different names.

Knowing this, I was curious as to what might be experienced in a great Egyptian temple that embodied the Hathor-Isis transpersonal force. It happened, but not in the way I expected.

After our tour of the big Hathor temple, I walked around and behind the huge walls of the building where I spied a smaller, ruined structure fashioned of large eroding stone blocks glowing yellow in the late afternoon light. On asking our guide about it, I was told it was the remains of a shrine dedicated to Isis.

The building appeared deserted, even neglected, compared to its monumental companion, yet I felt compelled to approach it. I climbed the steps along one side and stepped onto the shadowed stone platform from which two empty doorways entered into the dark interior of the shrine itself. Both doorways were guarded by iron bars with two locked gates. As I peered through the bars, I could see that the rooms were empty except for the reliefs carved into the walls. There was a niche at the back of the larger room that was empty too, its statuary and treasured power objects long gone to raiders and tomb robbers. I was by myself, though I could feel an unmistakable sense of someone or something there. It was elusive at first, coming and going, just there at the edge of my awareness. I glanced carefully around. I was alone on the ruined portico, and there was no one else in proximity to the shrine.

I sat down in the shade, my back against the wall of the shrine, and I closed my eyes. I entered into what I think of as the meditative state of shamanic consciousness. For long moments, I just sat still, my eyes closed, calming my mind, erasing my thoughts, allowing the inner mystical state to slowly expand within me. It was then that I felt it again, a definite presence.

On impulse, my hands felt for the zipper on my small waist pack, and my fingers extracted a glass crow bead, a blue one, my signature offering. I held it to my lips, eyes still closed, then breathed my prayer to the lady Isis through the hole in the bead, using it as the doorway into the transpersonal realm, offering to her my love along with an account of who I was and my intentions for being there in her shrine.

I waited, holding the bead between my fingers, savoring the moment, then I cracked an eye and tossed the bead through the iron bars into the darkness of her shrine. I smiled, my ritual complete. Then I braced myself against the ancient stone wall behind my back and accessed the high-frequency brain-wave states I have described in some detail in my Spiritwalker trilogy.

(Allow me to say that I don't really know what it is that I do in these moments. I just intend it and the rest happens. It is part of what I have described as personal transformation.)

Blood began to hiss in my ears as the exquisite pressure arrived accompanied by the uncontrollable vibrations of the expanding visionary state. I felt the familiar soaring feeling increase . . . increase, growing incrementally as my body commenced to shake as I built up my connection with the mind-blowing energy field that Obi-Wan Kenobi called the Force and that the Polynesians call *mauri ora*. All authentic mystics have experienced it. I believe it is the power of the life force itself.

The transcendent state suddenly expanded within me and possessed me, and while my body began to vibrate, gripped in the invisible fist of power, it was as though a window in my mind had opened and a feeling of utter tranquility enveloped me. Abruptly and unexpectedly, I descended into darkness, into the velvety blackness of the great void. My conscious awareness was just there, in that place of utter stillness and awesome silence . . . a state in which all that ever was and all that will ever be is unified in the now, in a state of waiting, of is-ness, of being-ness.

This place is the state of where the greatest creative work of the universes is manifested. I did not know this when I wrote about my first experience of this place in *Spiritwalker*. And then, in response to my intention, I suddenly perceived her—the goddess Isis, but not as some symbolic woman form or humanized feminine personification.

A brilliance appeared in the darkness of the void, a radiance that expanded into a moving, flowing mass of effervescent cobalt blue light that was alive and shimmering. It had depth, like staring into crystal clear blue water, but it had no boundaries, and yet in a flash, I was in this blueness. It was all around me. It merged with me, or I had merged with it, so that in those moments I was the blueness. Deity Mysticism. And I was immediately aware that it possessed a vast intelligence far beyond my own. Simultaneously, her awareness and mine became one.

This is the mystic experience at its absolute best, and it is available to all who choose to achieve it, those who have experienced personal transformation. During this extraordinary encounter, the soaring sensations that gripped my physical body amped up to an entirely new level in response to her connection with me. And there was more.

I have said that this was a very warm afternoon. However, in those moments, I suddenly experienced a sudden coolness, like when you open a refrigerator and the cold internal air flows down and outward over your bare feet. This is what enveloped me in those moments of vision. I was literally enfolded by a coolness, like a river of blue cold air flowing over me in a wave, engulfing me in a field in which I knew what she knew, I felt what she felt, I thought what she thought, and in that state the goddess and I were one.

I was perceiving her on the one hand as her "light beyond the form," and I was experiencing her directly as "the formless beyond the light." And there was no doubt in those moments that she—the Isis/mother goddess energy—was real. Then the vision faded as I heard the footsteps of others approaching the shrine and my focus shifted from "there" back to "here." Yet the resonance of her grace persisted for several days until I was fully drawn back into my world.

Almost six years later, on December 9, 2008, I was back at her shrine behind the temple at Dendara. As I ascended the stone steps of her shrine behind the Hathor temple once again, I was expectant, to say the least. And this time, much to my surprise, there was an Egyptian guard in a turban and galabeya (the traditional cotton robe), complete with moustache, who smiled and looked directly into my soul. Then he unlocked the gates on both entrances to the shrine. I smiled and tipped him and he graciously withdrew, leaving me alone.

Wary, I entered the inner recesses of her shrine for the first time, allowing my mind to slowly settle. This time my wife, Jill, was there as well, waiting outside with some of the others in our group, granting me the space to just be with Isis. Then, as before, I fished in my waist pack—for three blue beads this time—one for me and one for Jill, and one for Sandra Ingerman in New Mexico who had asked me to convey her love to the goddess. I breathed my prayer through the beads, then still standing

I placed my hands on the wall, on both sides of the niche in which her statue once stood, and closed my eyes. I offered my prayer for me and for my wife, and for my good friend as well. I felt my fingers discover a deep crack in the stone wall, so I tucked the three blue beads there, and then I accessed the high-frequency visionary state.

Once again, I felt her presence expand within my fully aroused consciousness. There was no doubt, no question. It felt familiar this time, and I became aware that this was an old transpersonal connection spanning many lifetimes. In response to this insight, glimpses of the past began to flow through my mind. They were memories, of course, but they were not the memories of Hank Wesselman. *Then whose memories are they?* I thought as I watched them, and then the answer came. They were being downloaded from my immortal oversoul field—my personal spiritual aspect that resides in the same transpersonal realm in which the Isis field exists. They were originating from my self-aspect in which all of my former selves are archived.

I watched enthralled as image after image emerged within my mind, like slides projected upon a screen, flowing with mystical vitality, power, and life force. As before, the radiance of her light was a brilliant blue hue, and her awareness conveyed a sense of utter acceptance and a distinctly feminine amusement.

The goddess was amused at my astonished state and my response to what was flowing through my mind, and through hers. Then the imagery suddenly shifted as an issue abruptly emerged from within the memories stored within my own Hank Wesselman mind. It was a recent memory of an event—one of the great betrayals of my life—that had happened only just the year before.

For many months I had suffered great anguish and grief over this event. I relived it even as I stood there in her shrine, my hands braced against the wall, my body shaking with the force of her presence. And then as before, the temperature abruptly shifted as her cool field once again swept down and engulfed me. I was bathed in the cold radiance of her grace, and in response I felt my grief over this terrible betrayal ebbing away, slowly dissolving in her blue light . . . going . . . going . . . and then gone.

I understood in those moments that when we are dealing with grief, or with issues of violation and betrayal, Isis is the one to whom we must journey, that Isis is the transpersonal ally who graces us with the qualities of forgiveness and reconciliation. I also understood in those moments that my lady Isis and the Himalayan bodhisattva Avalokiteshvara, the Chinese goddess Kwan Yin, and the Japanese spirit Kwannon are one and the same.

With this insight, I felt, rather than saw, her smile.

Then once again, I heard the voices of some of my companions approaching the shrine. My awareness shifted, and the feelings of force that had held me in their grip simply faded away. I was also aware that I had had a major healing from Isis, and the edge of anger that I had carried for over a year around that great betrayal was gone.

My gratitude was beyond description.

BEING OF SERVICE

D o experiences with transpersonal forces, such as my encounter with Isis (see chapter 9), support or refute the so-called law of attraction? Well, that depends on your frame of reference. A friend and I were discussing the matter recently, and we came to the conclusion that the law of attraction as presented in New Age teachings is basically a form of escapism. The law of attraction resonates with people who have complex lives and who don't know how to deal with their complicated problems. What they want is to have simple, easy solutions so that their problems can be resolved by some ideal replacement.

What's less than good is that the law of attraction tends to blame the one who is suffering for their predicaments: if you think negative thoughts, you will attract negative experiences. All this so-called law says is, "Just think everything better and everything will be okay." But you can't just think beautiful thoughts to resolve your problems, although those issues may become clearer through the practice of meditation. What is more effective than indulging in wishful thinking and expecting everything to get better is to roll up your sleeves and take positive action. As my friend wisely observed, "Actions speak louder than attraction."

Engaging with the compassionate archetypal higher forces that are poised to help us, as shamanists do, is taking action, and things do have a way of shifting if the field is favorable. And remember (once again), dealing with spirits is not about worship. It's about relationship. The energy is not one-way. It's rotary. As they are in service to us, so we may also be in service to them.

The focus of your intentionality is always important as you engage in journeywork. Are you seeking connection with your spirit helpers to acquire or achieve something material, or are you doing the work from a place of being of service for the highest good for yourself and those around you? If the former, then you may be stuck in the negative polarity of your body soul's desires and this may influence the outcome accordingly. If the latter, you are in the positive polarity, in alignment with your oversoul's dreams, and good things may happen.

In an article in *Shambala Sun,* Rachel Naomi Remen, MD, observed that being of service is quite different from helping and fixing. "When you help, you see life as weak. When you fix, you see life as broken. When you serve, you see life as whole," she wrote. "Service," she went on, "rests on the basic premise that the nature of life is sacred, that life is a holy mystery that has an unknown purpose. When we serve, we know that we belong to life and to that purpose. From the perspective of service, we are all connected. All suffering is like my suffering and all joy is like my joy. The impulse to serve emerges naturally from these perceptions."[1]

This is an interesting perspective, isn't it? In this regard, allow me to offer some wonderful words that were shared with me many years ago by Hale Makua. They were conveyed through our personal conversations during the last part of his life:

> Know that when you find love within its pure form,
> you are not confined; you are not finite. When you

have found that pure love, you have found your eternity. And in this eternity, the wind of the present moment offers all lessons.

It is at this moment that we must decide whether the illusion that creates judgment is to be seen as appropriate. It is now that we are faced with a choice: whether to judge or whether to appreciate, whether to ask for service or whether to be an agent of infinite service.

If we are able to let our love be free to ride the wind of spirit, we are always following the plan that we have laid out for our own soul's growth. Know that this is the density wherein we make decisions about the nature of everything, including all those about us and, of necessity, ourselves.

Within the understanding that comes to us in response, we can then choose how we shall serve that Mystery that created us and the All-That-Is.

Those who have read *The Bowl of Light* may recall that Makua once referred to me as a "wanderer," equating me with a tropical fish, the Achilles tang (*Acanthurus achilles*), known in Hawaiian as *paku'iku'i*—the wanderer. He revealed that the wanderers are those who come into life from the "higher densities" (his term) and who have chosen to incarnate here in order to be in service to others. The wanderers still have to remember who they are, he said, and part of the concern is that sometimes they do not awaken because of the extraordinary power of the masters of deception. The wanderers are here to awaken themselves first, he concluded, and then to help awaken others. And how many wanderers are loose in this world at this time, I wonder?

Makua felt that our job (as wanderers) is to be as a lighthouse, shining in the darkness. He added that we have to be careful not to burn others with our light, but rather allow them to be drawn toward our light like moths to a candle so that we might be of service to those who come toward us willingly. Now, many years after his passing, he lives clearly in my memory as the enigmatic and loving wise old sage, the magnetic chief to whom others were drawn because of the quality of his vibration rather than the volume of his rhetoric. He exemplified the ability to "walk his talk" so that others could see the effect of spirit conducting its wonderful work through him. He was a lighthouse who revealed the luminous path of being in service to all.

Makua's words, and those of Rachel Naomi Remen, reveal the nature of our practice as modern mystics. We are always in service to the Mystery and to our own uniquely human species and to the world soul who dreamed us. This is our job, and each of us does it in our own way. No matter what ideologies may separate us in this great game, the message is what matters, not the messenger. As I wrote in *Visionseeker*, "Those in thirst need water, not the faucet," and the message is always and forever the same—that in the love and the light of the infinite Originator, we are all manifested expressions of the One.[2]

THE CULTURAL
REVITALIZATION MOVEMENT

There is a social phenomenon known to anthropologists as a cultural revitalization movement. Such an event often occurs when members of an oppressed culture seek to revitalize themselves by reaching back into the past, often to reconnect with the spirits of their ancestors to bring forward into the present those things that have been lost and that once sustained them, especially lost spiritual knowledge. The indigenous peoples know that there is a relationship between knowledge and power. And when you recover lost knowledge, you are restoring power to individuals, even to entire tribal groups.

Drawing from my knowledge of anthropology and my conversations with the anthropologist Michael Harner years ago, I see a classic example of a cultural revitalization movement in the Ghost Dance religion of the 1890s. This was also known as the Father Dance or the Prophet's Dance and sometimes as the Dream Dance. It was initiated by a Northern Paiute American Indian prophet and shaman named Wovoka who had a near-death experience and was drawn into the Upper Worlds. When Wovoka returned from his visionary journey, he related that he had been given a dance of unusual movements by the ancestors, a dance that could help renew the earth. He said that he had been told to bring it back to the people. The purpose of the dance was to help people access the spirit worlds to meet with a family ancestor or a more distant spiritual ancestor to recover lost knowledge or a ritual. At that time the American Indians had been subjected to genocide, and most of the elders, those who knew the ceremonies, prayers, songs, and magic had all been killed.

When performed, the Ghost Dance was a kind of people's divinatory shamanism in which the whole community participated instead of only the shaman. It had the effect of causing participants to collapse in an altered state of consciousness in which they connected with the spirits. Wovoka proclaimed that the dance was to help bring the people back to peace and harmony and to revitalize (re-enchant) nature. The dance spread rapidly across North America, and many tribal people adapted and changed it according to their needs. In accordance with the ancestors' admonition that the dance was for everybody, regardless of ethnicity, people came from all over, including many Mormons who considered Wovoka as a manifestation of Christ. It was a last desperate attempt to bring forward once again the rituals and prayers, the ceremonies and the power, to bring back the buffalo, but most of all to revitalize the American Indian cultures that were on the verge of extinction.[1]

Today, more than a hundred years later, we find ourselves in a similar situation as we consider the magnitude of the challenges we face in our immediate future. It is easy to feel overwhelmed as we consider the nature of our political, social, economic, religious, and personal issues. On top is the certainty of catastrophic climate change and what that will bring to all of us worldwide, for Mother Nature (Sophia) does not negotiate. She responds.

Then there is the enormous transfer of wealth to the upper strata of society, which is leading to the progressive enslavement of the poor and working-class families and the elimination of the middle class. On a broader scale, half the world's population lives in conditions of abject poverty, which is simply appalling. In a sentence, we have a crisis of leadership on our hands, and the polyglot mosaic of what could now be called "Western culture" simply must adapt and change—or die.

With the current shift into the next cycle of ages, there is now a general agreement among our visionaries that a great healing has become possible for humanity, individually and collectively, and this is said to be so for our planet too. Many, including me, feel strongly that this will involve a re-enchantment—a re-enchantment of ourselves and a re-enchantment of nature. There is once again hope for a different outcome—hope for a future filled with direction, good intention, and harmony, hope for a rebirth of love, personal health and well-being, and hope for a renewed sense of satisfaction and security. As Desmond Tutu has wisely observed, "Hope is being able to see that there is light despite all of the darkness."[2]

Consciously or unconsciously, we are all participating in this rebirthing, and our collective spiritual essence has the potential to weave together a new foundation for the human experience, as revealed in Max Zeller's dream (see chapter 7), transcending any and all limitations, encouraging us to go within ourselves where we may rediscover deep levels of inspiration for living. Inspiration is sourced into us by our god-self, and we simply must choose to engage with and embody our oversoul's dreams, for our life lessons are always and forever about choice. To do this requires that we take courage because change is what people seem to fear most.

THOUGHTS FROM
A HAWAIIAN KAHUNA

Toward the end of his life, I remember the Hawaiian elder Hale Makua saying more than once that when we accept the calling that comes from "the deep" within us and we step onto the path of the inspired visionary once again, there is no knowledge of what will follow. He observed that at the onset, we have little understanding of what it means to participate in the shamans' numinous worlds, for our lives have yet to be tested against the challenges that the shamanic life may present to us in our initiatory experiences. For those used to being able to predict and to some degree direct the course of their lives, this can be problematic, but this is also part of what it means to be living in a time of new beginnings.

I have come to understand that the ever-growing interest in the ancient yet curiously modern spiritual path of the shaman is very much a part of our own revitalization movement. Once we have had that direct transformative experience of the spiritual dimensions and the beings who reside within them, everything changes for the better.

Makua knew that when we come into relationship with our spirit guardians, we discover a constant dialogue between the physical and nonphysical worlds, and this may be illuminating, even thrilling, though it may also be frightening. As many have discerned, the borderland between a spiritual emergence and a spiritual emergency can be elusive, as most of us have not been raised in families in which communication with spirits is part of the given. However, the authentic experience of interdimensional contact can and does present us with levels of guidance that are advanced both in scope as well as intention.

Makua often observed that we are meant to work with dimensions of life far greater than those that can be seen or appreciated in physical form. In doing so, we come to understand that humankind is responsible not only for the quality of life on planet Earth, but equally for the quality of our thoughts, emotions, and actions affecting each other, as well as the life force in all its manifestations. And it is through this collective planetary interaction that we all discover how important and precious each of us is to the greater whole.

As we move into the new era, life in all its beautiful and challenging aspects is morphing into new patterns. At the personal level, our life lessons continue to challenge us as our souls unfold and grow. Those who choose to walk the shaman's path discover that those lessons can be enormously enhanced in response to our relationships with our helping spirits and spirit teachers. For as I have observed, once we are in connection with our spirit friends, we've got power in our corner.

Makua spoke often of how this experience may also touch us deeply where we are most vulnerable, for as we progress, we continue to be exposed to the multidimensional worlds of other people's fears, desires, needs, and conscious and unconscious attitudes. Our reactions to their belief systems and emotional states can bring us moments of inner turmoil, as well as opportunities to both change and heal.

Along the way we discover that we are rarely asked to handle more than that from which we can immediately learn. Our lessons and the lessons of others seem to be offered to us in direct relation to the issues we need to see most clearly. In response, we are progressively led into the higher spiritual levels of our being. These inner recesses are calm and filled with a soothing energy, in contrast to the constant edgy crises, demands, and agitations of daily life. And they can be accessed through shamanic meditation.

When we become aware of our oversoul's dreams, Makua affirmed that the spiritual light within our hearts, though very private and very tender, can also be amazingly persistent in drawing our attention back to our own true selves and to the special qualities that are ours and ours alone. We discover that our connection with our spirit guardians offers the solace and the healing energy necessary for us to grow so that we understand who we really are and where we are in our long voyage across space and time. And as we continue to connect with our inner sources of wisdom, power, and healing, he said, we are constantly encouraged to re-evaluate our lives, and we may experience inner stirrings that urge us to move in strange and unfamiliar directions. These stirrings flow into us from our oversoul as causal impulses that increase our opportunities to grow and learn and become more than we were.

In *The Bowl of Light*, Makua revealed that when we are in alignment with our oversoul's dreams we are on the path of our destiny. This seems to be what the whole game of life is all about: a co-creative relationship between our transpersonal oversoul self and our personal embodied self. This relationship is and forever will be about a partnership through which we realize the presence of the divine within ourselves and within all things. This partnership offers each of us the gift of freedom, our personal sovereignty from which all other gifts flow. Yet true partnership can be achieved only by whole beings who retain their separateness, their uniqueness, even when it involves union with the divine. When we step onto the shaman's path of direct revelation, we have the opportunity to experience this fully, and in doing so our life may expand in unexpected directions.

As we move beyond those seemingly safe places and faith-based belief systems that can and do sustain us in the short term, we enter unknown territories through direct experience where we may encounter other worlds and other ways, including universal wisdom and the energy of love that will carry us through our most vigorous and painful of journeys across time and into what Makua called the Sea of Light.

Finally, Makua revealed that the best way to measure how far we have come or how much we have learned is to look back to where we began in order to assess the significance and magnitude of our development and progress. Those who walk the shaman's path are involved with the conscious teachings that come from nature, our mother planet, Earth. This means that in receiving these teachings, we interact with the whole.

Shamanists know that this planetary whole that we call Earth is both conscious and sentient and that the soul of our world is located within the biosphere, the part that contains life. Earth has a physical presence (planetary body), a means of processing information (planetary mind), and a commitment to a divine path (planetary soul). It has a purpose, as well as issues of delusion versus truth, just as we do, and we discover through direct experience that Earth is taught, as are we, by the collective energetic streaming of the life force that Makua called *mauri ora*. The word *evolution* simply means "change," and change, as we all discover, is the texture of the universe that is in no way punitive or disciplinary, but rather creative and growth producing. The state of change is ongoing and continually redirects our attention toward that which is true versus that which is transient. In this sense, the geosphere and the biosphere of nature are the collective fields that are always and forever true. And our human cultures? Hard to say. They are restless, always changing, always shifting, and much of what makes them up is questionable.

When we consciously form our thoughts into intentions devoted to goodness and direct our intentions into appropriate actions accordingly, this allows us to live life to our fullest capacity, existing for our own greatest good and for the greatest good of the whole. Makua often said (wistfully) that it is only when we are in the positive polarity that we may connect with our spirit helpers and spirit teachers, with our ancestors, and with those higher organizing intelligences who will help us grow into our full and complete magnificence. This is what is meant by our re-enchantment, an experience that will contribute, person by person, to the revitalization of our culture and our world.

It is in this way that we can experience the joy of being in service to each other and to the world soul, Sophia, and in doing so we may become what Makua called Navigators of Light. This is the path upon which we may choose to walk as we journey into the next cycle of ages and out toward the distant, dusty horizons of the unknown.

And it is there, just there, that we often find ourselves in very good company.

POSTSCRIPT

It would be appropriate, I think, to conclude our ruminations with a few wise words from the great physicist Albert Einstein, who had a mystic side of which few are aware. He included this observation in a letter to Oscar Juliusburger on September 29, 1947, revealing that the master game was among the life games Einstein played.

> People like you and me, though mortal, of course,
> do not grow old no matter how long we live. What
> I mean is that we never cease to stand like curious
> children before the great Mystery into which we were
> born. This interposes a distance between us and all
> that is unsatisfactory in the human sphere—and this
> is no small matter.[1]

No small matter indeed. And to you, the reader, welcome to the club. There are no dues, no committee meetings—just reverence.

THE ROLE OF THE AUTHENTIC SHAMANIC TEACHER

I n the Western world today, more and more nontribal West-erners are seeking out a teacher of shamanism; as a result, increasing numbers of shamanic teachers are now appearing on the screen. But how do we ensure that we will be drawn to an authentically initiated individual who will serve us well?

In the beginning, many of us decide to seek out teachers in the indigenous world, often through participating in travel groups or tours into remote regions like Peru or the Ama-zon. These tours, which are usually accompanied or led by an acknowledged or self-proclaimed expert, can be intense, excit-ing, and life-changing. However, we frequently discover that these travel adventures lack an ongoing connection to facilitate developing our shamanic skills and abilities.

Some of us seek out indigenous spiritual elders closer to home, yet we usually discover that there are very few of them now who still know the old traditions and fewer still who may be inclined to share their spiritual wisdom with outsiders. Some of us are lucky, though, and find our way into relationship with an elder like Hale Makua, who has chosen to extend their knowledge to everyone, regardless of culture, race, or ethnicity—and this is what it means to be an authentic medicine person.

Then there are the growing numbers of spiritual seekers who become aware of the shaman's path through the published works of individuals who have "spent time" with indigenous peoples or who have had visionary experiences themselves. Some find their way into relationship with these individuals who offer knowledge as well as experiential training in seminars and workshops at institutes and conference centers. The hands-on experiential workshop with an accomplished teacher offers opportunities for intense immersion in the shaman's worldview and practice. These structured settings provide tools and techniques designed to bring us into an enhanced connection with our spirit helpers, our spirit teachers, and our Spirit Guides, creating a good working foundation for our own practice.

In the shaman's world it is always understood, however, that the real teachers are found on the other side of the mirror. Only the spirits can convey true teaching as well as initiation to the shamanic practitioner. Accordingly, the job of the authentic shamanic teacher is to facilitate this connection.

Once the shamanic aspirant has been brought into relationship with their helping and teaching spirits, the role of the outer teacher is essentially done. Yet it is also true that many initiates return to work with a singular teacher in serial training workshops in order to deepen their practice in specific areas, such as working with ancestral spirits, soul retrieval, transpersonal healing, or exploring the dimensional realities of the other worlds.

In doing so, we discover that the ancient methodologies of the shaman, developed across tens of millennia by our Stone Age ancestors, are the birthright of all human beings everywhere. As we have observed, it is not required that you be a Zulu or a Siberian, a Mayan or a Hawaiian, an Aboriginal or Lakota to practice shamanism. The practice, the core method, is essentially the same the world over. It belongs to us all.

APPENDIX 2

THE THREE QUALITIES
OF THE SHAMANIC TEACHER

Allow me to share a few insights for those looking for a teacher, as well as for those who feel drawn to become shamanic teachers themselves. In doing so, I am speaking from more than thirty years of apprenticeship in this timeless tradition, a period during which I have been in relationship with many teachers in the outer world, both Western and indigenous, as well as with inner teachers in spirit.

Under their wise tutelage, I practiced the shaman's craft for more than twelve years before I became a shamanic teacher. At that point, I did not simply create workshops based on what I had been taught and then market them to my community, proclaiming myself as a shamanic practitioner and teacher. Rather, members of my community, hearing or knowing of my interests by word of mouth, began to ask me to speak at gatherings.

Often these events took the form of one- to two-hour talks accompanied by experiential journeywork or a healing ritual, usually in someone's living room on a Sunday afternoon, sometimes followed by a potluck meal. No money was involved, and these informal events continued for several years until my first book, *Spiritwalker: Messages from the Future*, was published. Then the invitations to speak and teach began to come from conferences and institutes. I never sent in resumes, approaching this well-known institute or that conference committee with a proposal for a talk or a workshop. I waited to be invited, and this remains my protocol to this day.

The big question still lurks in the shadows for consideration, however: How do you know when a shamanic teacher is authentic? How do you know whether this well-published author or that unknown (yet fervent) individual has been authentically initiated and trained? This is most important, for if there is one thing that spiritual seekers in the transformational community are looking for, it is authenticity, and here, from my experience, are some pointers you might consider.

The first thing that I look for in a spiritual teacher is humility. If someone stands up in front of a group and announces that they are a shaman or a kahuna, that's your first red flag. No authentic shaman, or kahuna for that matter, ever claims the title. It just isn't done. All authentic shamans know that the power to which they have access is on loan from the spirits. They also know that when a practitioner becomes a little too full of themselves, proclaiming themselves to be a shaman, a kahuna, or a healer, this is the quickest way for them to lose connection with that power. There are exceptions, but they are rare. Accordingly, all authentic shamans tend to be very humble people. Sometimes they will describe themselves and what they do using the term *shamanic practitioner*. This is acceptable and is aligned with humility. In this book, I have also suggested that we may use the term *shamanist* in the same way that folks may call themselves Buddhists or Taoists.

The second quality I watch for is reverence. In this case, reverence refers to an active respect that is extended to everyone and everything, regardless of who and what they are. No judgment. If you find yourself in a group with a teacher who is autocratic, demanding, condemning, or rigid, you might reconsider your commitment to that teacher. If you find yourself in a travel group where the leader treats the locals unkindly or with disrespect, this is not a favorable sign.

The third quality I watch for is self-discipline. If you have found yourself with a spiritual teacher who is arrogant, who expresses themselves through proclamation and pontification, or if you have found yourself in the presence of someone who seduces you with wonderful stories and accounts that may or may not be true, you're probably in the wrong place. If you hear through the grapevine that a well-published, well-traveled, and well-known teacher violates the boundaries of their students, specifically sexually, you would be better served to find a more trustworthy individual to help facilitate your spiritual growth.

That said, allow me to add that my wife, Jill, and I do encourage our workshop participants to work with as many accomplished and authentically initiated teachers as possible. In addition to their teachings, these individuals bring us into enhanced connection with each other, creating community. Through interconnection and cooperation with others of similar orientation and training, our experience broadens, our abilities sharpen to become more refined, and our knowledge deepens to become wisdom.

In the wise words of Hale Makua, when we walk on the shamanic path of direct revelation, "we are to love all that we see with humility, live all that we feel with reverence, and know all that we possess with discipline."

This is a path with heart—a path that reflects our honor.

NOTES

1 THE ENCHANTMENT AND RE-ENCHANTMENT

1. See Lyall Watson, *Lightning Bird: One Man's Journey into Africa* (New York: Simon & Schuster/Touchstone, 1983).
2. Peter Matthiessen and Eliot Porter (photographs), *The Tree Where Man Was Born/The African Experience,* 1st ed. (New York: E. P. Dutton, 1972), 391.

2 SHAMANISM AND THE SEAT OF INITIATION

1. Hank Wesselman, *The Bowl of Light: Ancestral Wisdom from a Hawaiian Shaman* (Boulder, CO: Sounds True, 2011), 192.
2. Robert S. de Ropp, *The Master Game: Pathways to Higher Consciousness Beyond the Drug Experience* (New York: Delta Press, 1968), 12, 19.

3 SOPHIA'S DREAM

1. John Lamb Lash, *Not in His Image: Gnostic Vision, Sacred Ecology, and the Future of Belief* (White River Junction, VT: Chelsea Green Publishing, 2006), 144.
2. Ibid., 113, 169.
3. Hank Wesselman, *Visionseeker: Shared Wisdom from the Place of Refuge* (Carlsbad, CA: Hay House, 2002), 287.
4. Lash, *Not in His Image*, 176.
5. Stephen Hawking, *A Brief History of Time*, 10th anniversary ed. (New York: Bantam, 1998), 38.
6. Lash, *Not in His Image*, 172–76.

7. James Hansen et al., "Global Warming in the Twenty-First Century: An Alternative Scenario," *Proceedings of the National Academy of Sciences of the United States of America* 97, no. 8 (2000): 9875–880.

8. James Hansen et al., "Ice Melt, Sea Level Rise, and Superstorms: Evidence from Paleoclimate Data, Climate Modeling, and Modern Observations that 2 °C Global Warming Could Be Dangerous," *Atmospheric Chemistry and Physics*, 16 (2016): 3761–812, doi:10.5194/acp-16-3761-2016.

4 THE EVOLUTION OF RELIGION

1. Colin M. Turnbull, *The Forest People*, reissue ed. (1961; New York: Simon & Schuster/Touchstone, 1987).

2. Emile Durkheim, *The Elementary Forms of Religious Life* (1912; repr., CreateSpace, 2014).

3. Edward B. Tylor, *Primitive Culture: Researches Into the Development of Mythology, Philosophy, Religion, Language, Art, and Custom*, 2 vols. (1871; repr., Nabu Press, 2010).

4. R. R. Marett, *The Threshold of Religion* (Oxford: Clarendon Press, 1909).

5. Guy E. Swanson, *The Birth of the Gods: The Origin of Primitive Beliefs* (Ann Arbor: University of Michigan Press, 1960).

6. Graham Hancock, *Supernatural: Meetings with the Ancient Teachers of Mankind*, rev. ed. (New York: Disinformation Books, 2006).

7. Rick Strassman, *DMT: The Spirit Molecule—A Doctor's Revolutionary Research into the Biology of Near-Death and Mystical Experiences* (Rochester, VT: Park Street Press, 2000), 54.

8. See Ralph Waldo Emerson, "The Over-Soul," essay 9 in *Essays—First Series* (1841).

9. Hancock, *Supernatural*, chap 15.

10. Ibid.

5 ENCOUNTERS WITH THE NORTH WIND

1. George MacDonald, *At the Back of the North Wind* (1871; repr., CreateSpace, 2012).

6 THE NEW MYSTERIES

1. Lash, *Not in His Image*, 215–23.

2. Wesselman, *The Bowl of Light*, 146.

3. Michael Newton, *Journey of Souls: Case Studies of Life Between Lives* (Woodbury, MN: Llewellyn Publications, 1994); *Destiny of Souls: New Case Studies of Life Between Lives* (Woodbury, MN: Llewellyn, 2000); Linda Backman, *Bringing Your Soul to Light: Healing Through Past Lives and the Time Between* (Woodbury, MN: Llewellyn, 2009); *The Evolving Soul: Spiritual Healing Through Past Life Regression* (Woodbury, MN: Llewellyn, 2014).

4. Arthur Caswell Parker, *The Code of Handsome Lake, the Seneca Prophet* (Albany, NY: New York State Education Department, 1913; repr., London: Forgotten Books, 2008).

5. Oprah Winfrey, "Soul to Soul: Exploring the Big Questions with Dr. Wayne Dyer," *SuperSoul Sunday*, OWN, March 26, 2012.

6. Carolyn Boyes-Watson and Kay Pranis, *Heart of Hope: A Guide for Using Peacemaking Circles to Develop Emotional Literacy, Promote Healing & Build Healthy Relationships* (St. Paul, MN: Living Justice Press, 2010).

7. "Albert Einstein & Rabindranath Tagore on the Nature of Reality," Mindpod Network, mindpodnetwork.com/albert-einstein-rabindranath-tagore-nature-reality/.

8. Alex Grey, *Sacred Mirrors: The Visionary Art of Alex Grey* (Rochester, VT: Inner Traditions, 1990).

9. Thomas Moore, *A Religion of One's Own: A Guide to Creating a Personal Spirituality in a Secular World*, repr. ed. (New York: Penguin Group, Gotham, 2015), 204–5.

10. Philip Freeman, *The Philosopher and the Druids: A Journey Among the Ancient Celts* (New York: Simon & Schuster, 2008).

11. Dalai Lama XIV, Tsong-ka-pa, and Jeffrey Hopkins, *Deity Yoga: In Action and Performance Tantra*, repr. ed. (Ithaca, NY: Snow Lion, 1987); see also Jeffrey Hopkins, *The Tantric Distinction: A Buddhist's Reflection on Compassion and Emptiness*, rev. ed. (Somerville, MA: Wisdom Publications, 2013).

12. Tom Harpur, *The Pagan Christ: Recovering the Lost Light* (Toronto, CA: Thomas Allen Publishers, 2005), 27–48.

13. Ibid., 21–25; see also D. M. Murdock, *Christ in Egypt: The Horus-Jesus Connection* (Seattle: Stellar House Publishing, 2009).

14. Harpur, *The Pagan Christ*, 50–65.

15. Lash, *Not in His Image*, 146–48.

16. Ibid., 211–12.

17. Murdock, *Christ in Egypt*.

18. D. M. Murdock (as Acharya S), *The Christ Conspiracy: The Greatest Story Ever Sold* (Kempton, IL: Adventures Unlimited Press, 1999); *Suns of God: Krishna, Buddha, and Christ Unveiled* (Kempton, IL: Adventures Unlimited Press, 2004).

19. Michael Paulkovich, *No Meek Messiah: Christianity's Lies, Laws, and Legacy* (Annapolis, MD: Spillix LLC, 2013).

20. Joseph Atwill, *Caesar's Messiah: The Roman Conspiracy to Invent Jesus* (CreateSpace, 2011).

21. John G. Jackson, *Pagan Origins of the Christ Myth* (Austin, TX: American Atheist Press, 1989).

22. Yonassan Gershom, "Shamanism in the Jewish Tradition," in *Shamanism: An Expanded View of Reality*, ed. Shirley Nicolson (Wheaton, IL: Quest Books, 1987); see also Gershon Winkler, *Magic of the Ordinary: Recovering the Shamanic in Judaism* (Berkeley, CA: North Atlantic Books, 2003).

23. Harpur, *The Pagan Christ*, 21–23, 147.

24. Ibid., 23–24.

25. Patricia Storace, *Dinner with Persephone: Travels in Greece* (New York: Panthcon Books, 1996), 201.

26. C. J. De Catanzaro, *Symeon the New Theologian: The Discourses* (Mahwah, NJ: Paulist Press, 1980).

27. Ibid.

7 THE NEW DIRECTION

1. Max Zeller, *The Dream: The Vision of the Night* (Cheyenne, WY: Fisher King Press, 2015).

2. Ken Wilber, *One Taste: Daily Reflections on Integral Spirituality*, rev. sub. ed. (Boston: Shambhala, 2000).

8 THE MASTERS OF DECEPTION

1. Wesselman, *The Bowl of Light*, 224–26.

2. Lash, *Not in His Image*, 116, 123–27, 159–60, 162, 180, 182–85, 190–91, 192, 195, 197–98, 208, 210, 271–73, 275, 325, 331.

3. Ibid., 10–16, 54, 58, 105–22, 171, 180, 350–51.

4. Ibid., 76, 79–80, 90, 115, 117, 186–88, 210, 213, 228, 287–93, 296–97, 306, 354.

5. Ibid., 113–18, 160, 188, 192–93, 208, 220, 233, 237, 258, 260, 261, 283–87.

6. Paul Levy, *Dispelling Wetiko: Breaking the Curse of Evil* (Berkeley CA: North Atlantic Books, 2013).

7. Paul Levy's website, *Dispelling Wetiko*, awakeninthedream.com/dispelling-wetiko/.

8. C. G. Jung, *The Collected Works of C. G. Jung*. Vol. 11, *Psychology and Religion: West and East*, trans. R. F. C. Hull (New York: Pantheon Books, 1958).

9. Ibid.

10. Lash, *Not in His Image*, 229.

11. Jung, *Psychology and Religion*, 369. Thanks to C. Michael Smith for tracking down this quote.

12. Personal communication with C. Michael Smith, author of *Jung and Shamanism in Dialogue: Retrieving the Soul/Retrieving the Sacred* (Victoria, BC: Trafford Publishing, 2007). With regard to Edinger, Smith shares, "Jung moved his original concept from primordial images to a more platonic 'form of instinct' with luminosity." Smith gives a detailed analysis of the evolution of Jung's concept in his book.

9 PERSONAL TRANSFORMATION

1. I have written elsewhere about the phenomenon of spiritual unfolding and how it appears to happen in stages. See Hank Wesselman, "The Three Stages of Spiritual Unfolding," in *Shamanic Transformations: True Stories of the Moment of Awakening,* ed. Itzhak Beery (Rochester, VT: Destiny Books, 2015), 5–10; see also Wesselman, *The Bowl of Light*, 223–24.

10 Being of Service

1. Rachel Naomi Remen, "Helping, Fixing, or Serving?" *Shambhala Sun*, September 1, 1999, lionsroar.com/helping-fixing-or-serving.
2. Wesselman, *Visionseeker*, 292.

11 The Cultural Revitalization Movement

1. James Mooney, *The Ghost-dance Religion and the Sioux Outbreak of 1890* (Washington, DC: Government Printing Office, 1896; HardPress Publishing, 2012).
2. Deborah Solomon, "The Priest: Questions for Archbishop Desmond Tutu," *The New York Times Magazine*, March 4, 2010.

Postscript

1. Helen Dukas and Banesh Hoffmann, eds., *Albert Einstein, The Human Side: Glimpses from His Archives* (Princeton, NJ: Princeton University Press, 2013), 82.

Further Resources

Many who are drawn toward the shamanic path find themselves in search of books and teachings that may introduce them to and enhance their experience of this ancient tradition. I am always aware that because of geographic distance or financial considerations, many will never make it to one of my training workshops. So here are just a few resources that I—and my wife, Jill Kuykendall, as well as our colleague Sandra Ingerman—have created to place tools in the hands of our fellow mystics. All of these resources offer teachings that reveal what is possible, and some include CDs of shamanic drumming and rattling to help us engage in shamanic journeywork/meditation to expand our conscious awareness into those spirit worlds so familiar to shamans of all traditions.

Books on Shamanic Practice

Hank Wesselman, *The Journey to the Sacred Garden: A Guide to Traveling in the Spiritual Realms*. Carlsbad, CA: Hay House, 2003 (+ Shamanic Drumming CD). This is a small book with guidance for your own spiritual awakening, as well as exercises to bring you into connection with your spirit helpers and teachers through shamanic journeywork with assistance from the drumming CD included.

Hank Wesselman and Jill Kuykendall, *Spirit Medicine: A Guide to Healing in the Sacred Garden*. Carlsbad, CA: Hay House, 2004 (plus Shamanic Drumming CD). A small book that includes an overview of shamanic healing, including an examination of the three classic causes of illness and the four levels of shamanic healing, with exercises to create healing on your own behalf with the assistance of your healing spirits. It is a companion volume to *The Journey to the Sacred Garden*.

Sandra Ingerman and Hank Wesselman, *Awakening to the Spirit World: The Shamanic Path of Direct Revelation*. Boulder, CO: Sounds True, 2010 (+ Shamanic Drumming CD). An in-depth consideration of the shamanic tradition, with exercises to enhance shamanic practice as well as input from several other accomplished shamanic teachers. This book was awarded the gold medal as the best New Age (Body-Mind-Spirit) book of 2011 by the Independent Publisher Book Awards and voted the number one best Magic/Shamanism book in 2011 by the Coalition of Visionary Resources. It includes a CD for journeywork.

Hank Wesselman, *The Bowl of Light: Ancestral Wisdom from a Hawaiian Shaman*. Boulder, CO: Sounds True, 2011. This is a unique exploration into the mind and teachings of an authentic Hawaiian kahuna mystic in which the investigation of the three souls, the many levels of reality, and the ancestral grand plan is presented.

Sandra Ingerman, *Walking in Light: The Everyday Empowerment of a Shamanic Life*. Boulder, CO: Sounds True, 2014. An excellent compilation of the teachings of a modern Western shaman and medicine woman over the past several decades.

Sandra Ingerman, *Soul Retrieval: Mending the Fragmented Self*. San Francisco: HarperOne, 2006.

Sandra Ingerman, *Welcome Home: Following Your Soul's Journey Home*. San Francisco: HarperOne, 1994.

Other Books

Itzhak Beery, *The Gift of Shamanism: Visionary Power, Ayahuasca Dreams, and Journeys to the Other Realms*. Rochester, VT: Destiny Books, 2015. Another excellent overview of the practice of a modern Western shaman.

For an overview of the relationship between shamanism, Gestalt psychology, Platonic philosophy, and yoga, see Roberta Pughe, *Body as Sanctuary for Soul: An Embodied Enlightenment Practice*. Ashland, OR: White Cloud Press, 2015.

For those interested in working with the weather, see Nan Moss and David Corbin, *Weather Shamanism: Harmonizing Our Connection with the Elements*. Rochester, VT: Bear and Company, 2008.

Jane Roberts, *The Oversoul Seven Trilogy*. San Rafael, CA: Amber-Allen Publishing, 1995. These three books reveal through story the relationships between the spirit guide and the oversoul and between the oversoul and its embodiments.

There are also the autobiographical books in my Spiritwalker series. These volumes record an extraordinary story of how I was drawn into connection through deep trance with the mind, soul, and body of a man who may be one of my descendants and who lives in a slice of time roughly five thousand years after the collapse of Western civilization:

Hank Wesselman, *Spiritwalker: Messages from the Future*. New York: Bantam Books, 1995.

Hank Wesselman, *Medicinemaker: Mystic Encounters on the Shaman's Path*. New York: Bantam Books, 1998.

Hank Wesselman, *Visionseeker: Shared Wisdom from the Place of Refuge*. Carlsbad, CA: Hay House, 2001.

AUDIO AND VIDEO LEARNING PROGRAMS

Hank Wesselman and Jill Kuykendall, *The Spiritwalker Teachings: Journeys for the Modern Mystic*. A six-CD set that records much of our first-level, five-day Visionseeker workshop. Available through our website (sharedwisdom.com) as a direct download and through Amazon as a hard copy.

Hank Wesselman, *The Shaman's Path*, a self-guided video program available through Sounds True.

WEBSITES

For a schedule of Jill's and my shamanic training workshops, visit our website, Shared Wisdom (sharedwisdom.com).

Nan Moss offers workshops in weather shamanism. For more information, visit her website, shamanscircle.com.

Sandra Ingerman's website, Shamanic Teachers (shamanicteachers. com), is a great resource for those in search of a shamanic teacher or practitioner who Sandra has personally trained. See also her other website, sandraingerman.com.

ACKNOWLEDGMENTS

Many teachers, friends, and colleagues have contributed to my spiritual unfolding across the years. This esteemed fellowship includes both Westerners and indigenous people on this side of the mirror as well as my spirit teachers on the other. To all I express my deep gratitude and my great affection.

First and foremost among them is my lady Jill Kuykendall, my wife and the mother of our children, who has served as my most endearing, loving, and wise teacher for more than forty years. I bow to the light that she is and will continue to be.

The Hawaiian elder and kahuna Hale Kealohalani Makua and I had a unique friendship unlike any other in my life, from which I am still gleaning insights more than twelve years after his passing. We loved each other dearly, and I miss him greatly. All praises to him.

Michael Harner helped guide me back onto the ancient path more than thirty years ago when my initiations began. My subsequent friendship with Sandra Ingerman allowed us to create a wonderful award-winning book together and to serve as co-inspirators for the transformational community at large. All praises to them.

Then there are my students at the universities and colleges where I taught for so many years, as well the participants in my shamanic training workshops. I have learned as much from you as you acquired from me. In addition, the support I have received from the many institutions and venues where I have offered classes, seminars, and workshops has been pivotal in "getting the word out there" and connecting with members of the transformational community. They have all supported me in my attempts to be of service, and in response, much has been gained. All praises to them.

My literary agents Barbara Moulton and Candice Fuhrman have provided wise guidance for the publication of my books and all that came into being as a result. My undying gratitude and praises are extended to them. I also sing the praises of my editors Amy Rost and Jody Berman, as well as Jennifer Brown and Leslie Brown and the chief at Sounds True Publishing, Tami Simon. It is an honor to be included in your company of accomplished teachers. All praises to you.

Great gratitude is extended as well to my daughter Erica Wesselman for her early copyediting of this manuscript.

Then there is my readership, all of you kindred souls, known and unknown, spread out across our world, from whom I receive regular e-mails, letters, messages of encouragement, and gratitude for my unusual books. We're in this together and we should take courage, for we are traveling in very good company. We are creating a new story, a new cultural mythos, and a new world, and this is not a small thing. To you all, my very warmest *aloha nui loa* and my gratitude for your support.

Hank Wesselman
Honaunau, Hawai'i Island

ABOUT THE AUTHOR

Hank Wesselman, PhD, is an anthropologist and evolutionary biologist who earned his bachelor's and master's degrees in zoology from the University of Colorado at Boulder, and his doctoral degree in anthropology from the University of California at Berkeley. He served in the U.S. Peace Corps in Nigeria in the middle 1960s among the Yoruba people, where he first became interested in indigenous spiritual traditions. He has conducted expeditionary fieldwork since 1971 with several international research teams in search of answers to the mystery of human origins in the fossil beds of eastern Africa's Great Rift Valley. His fieldwork has allowed him to spend portions of his life with tribal peoples rarely if ever visited by outsiders. In addition to his scientific publications and his academic teaching in many universities and colleges, including the University of Hawai'i's West Hawai'i campus, the University of California at San Diego, California State University at Sacramento, American River College and Sierra College in Northern California, and Adeola Odutola College and Kiriji Memorial College in western Nigeria, he is the author of nine books on shamanism, including his critically acclaimed Spiritwalker trilogy, the award-winning *Awakening to the Spirit World: The Shamanic Path of Direct Revelation* (with Sandra Ingerman), *The Bowl of Light: Ancestral Wisdom from a Hawaiian Shaman*, and now *The Re-Enchantment: A Shamanic Path to a Life of Wonder*. A shamanic practitioner and teacher for more than twenty-five years and an apprentice in this mystical tradition for more than thirty, he offers experiential training workshops at various venues, including the Esalen Institute in California, the Breitenbush Conference

Center in northern Oregon, and the Omega Institute near New York City. He lives with his family on their organic farm in Honaunau, Hawai'i Island. Visit his website, Shared Wisdom (sharedwisdom.com).

About Sounds True

Sounds True is a multimedia publisher whose mission is to inspire and support personal transformation and spiritual awakening. Founded in 1985 and located in Boulder, Colorado, we work with many of the leading spiritual teachers, thinkers, healers, and visionary artists of our time. We strive with every title to preserve the essential "living wisdom" of the author or artist. It is our goal to create products that not only provide information to a reader or listener, but that also embody the quality of a wisdom transmission.

For those seeking genuine transformation, Sounds True is your trusted partner. At SoundsTrue.com you will find a wealth of free resources to support your journey, including exclusive weekly audio interviews, free downloads, interactive learning tools, and other special savings on all our titles.

To learn more, please visit SoundsTrue.com/freegifts or call us toll-free at 800.333.9185.